THREE COINS IN THE BIRDBATH

THREE COINS IN THE BIRDBATH

JACK SMITH

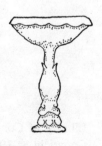

DOUBLEDAY & COMPANY, INC.
GARDEN CITY, NEW YORK
1965

Portions of this book in somewhat different form have appeared in The Los Angeles *Times*. The author is grateful to the publisher of that newspaper for permission to draw upon this material.

For Denny

PREFACE

Victoria Kling lives next door to Jack Smith. She is in the eighth grade at Florence Nightingale Junior High School, where she won second prize in an essay contest on "My Most Interesting Neighbor." Mr. Smith feels this work offers more insights into his character than he could himself. The publishers wish to thank Miss Kling for permission to use her essay as a preface to Mr. Smith's book.

Mr. Smith is my most interesting neighbor. He says we are living in cataclysmic times. Sometimes Mr. Smith scares me because he is always reading the encyclopedia and swearing.

Last Christmas he put a star up on his roof and he hit himself in the thumb with a screw driver. My mother says you shouldn't say things like he did when you're putting a star up on your roof.

I borrowed three potatoes from Mr. Smith once. It was a cataclysmic experience. My mother said what can you expect from a man who takes the name of the Lord in vain while putting a star up on his roof.

I like Mr. Smith anyway. He never gives me any candy. He says it isn't any good for my teeth.

He says my mother ought to grow her own potatoes like the pioneers did. My mother says Mr. Smith's only experience with the earth has been the growing of flowers of evil.

Mr. Smith has two nice boys but he doesn't like to work in the

garden. He is always telling Mrs. Smith if she wanted a gardener why
didn't she marry one. Sometimes he talks loud.

Mr. Smith's car is funny. It doesn't work some mornings. He gets
very mad. He says his boss won't believe him that his car isn't working
and will just think he is asleep listening to the news on the radio, the
way he does.

Mr. Smith is very generous, whatever the other people say. He
gave me a puppy once, but my mother wouldn't let me keep him.
She said beware of Greeks bearing gifts. The puppy had a white spot
on his nose. I was going to call him Balthazar. My mother says things
like that about Mr. Smith. He isn't really a Greek.

Mr. Smith doesn't like electricity. He is always going around turning off lights and lighting up candles. He says there is only so much
electricity in the world and why should one man get it all.

My mother says Mr. Smith is eccentric but probably harmless.
She says I am supposed to humor him. Mr. Smith is a very hard person to humor, especially when he is out of potatoes, and on Monday
mornings, when I had to borrow some sugar once. He says I am more
trouble than Southeast Asia.

Sometimes Mrs. Smith invites me to her house for dinner. I get to
wear a white dress. Mr. Smith always puts on the candles and turns
off the television. He says TV puts too much of a strain on the Hoover
Dam.

Things happen in our neighborhood that you wouldn't believe it if
they weren't true. The lady across the street's dog had puppies again.
Six this time and you would think she would stop. My mother says
she doesn't have any sense about her acquaintances. One of them is
brown with white spots. The other five are white with brown spots.
Nature is strange and lovely.

We have a new postman with glasses. He gets our mail mixed up
with Mr. Smith's so we get Mr. Smith's mail and he gets ours sometimes. My mother doesn't read Mr. Smith's mail but she says she can
tell that he gets letters from some peculiar people.

Whenever I get Mr. Smith's mail I have to take it to his house. The
postman comes before Mr. Smith goes to work in the morning so
when I ring the doorbell sometimes he is lying on his living room

floor reading the paper upside down and shaving with his electric shaver in his pajamas.

He says it relaxes him to shave on the floor. My mother says men should shave in the bathroom. Mr. Smith says he would be happy to shave in the bathroom but the door is always locked from the inside.

Mr. Smith had a package delivered to our house one morning which I got to take over to him and he was too sick even to shave lying down. He said he was too tired to shave and too tired to grow his beard. My mother says Mr. Smith is poisoned by his own thoughts.

Mr. Smith is always giving me good advice. He says I should read Shakespeare and eat of the lotus. He says I am too pretty to waste my beauty on the desert air and should quit wearing jeans and have my hair cut like the girls of France.

His pajamas are red with black stripes. He says he has to wear a gray suit to work and he at least ought to be able to wear bright colors when he is asleep in his own house.

Mr. Smith says I am too old and feminine to climb trees. I think I will have my hair cut like the girls of France if I can't have a puppy.

My ambition is to be an authoress like Emily Dickinson. Mr. Smith encourages me. He says he likes my stuff but I must be careful not to become too sophisticated.

My mother says I should not show Mr. Smith everything I write because I am not a child any more and might reveal myself subconsciously. She says I am reaching the age where I should hide something.

She says I am going through a period of transition, and my style is not fully developed. Mr. Smith says my development is marvelous, and he should know. He is extremely literary, for our block. Mr. Smith has visited many places and had many wonderful experiences, through books. He says I should read Edgar Allan Poe.

He says he is going to chuck everything some day and really go some place and do something, but I don't know. He always has car trouble, and I heard Mrs. Smith telling him one day that something had to be done about their lawn. Mr. Smith told her that if the Good Lord wanted grass in their yard He would have planted it there. Mr.

Smith is very religious. Mrs. Smith told him the Lord helps those who help themselves. He said that was a shibboleth.

My mother is a very wonderful woman, but she is quite old. She has lost interest in life. She won't even get her hair dyed. She says the Lord gave her the color her hair is, and she intends to keep it. In that way she is like Mr. Smith about his lawn.

Mr. Smith's hair is beginning to get gray at the temples. He says that when it is all gray, he will have the dignity he has always wanted. But it's a slow process. He says he is growing old waiting for his hair to turn gray.

Mr. Smith is an odd person, but I think he is very sincere. Sometimes he has pure wisdom. He was right about me getting too old to climb trees because I fell and cut my lip. Mr. Smith explained that when girls get to be my age their balance changes and they ought to stay on the ground and wear high heels.

Mr. Smith is a very superior neighbor, I think.

VICTORIA KLING
Grade 8-B
Florence Nightingale Jr. H.S.

CONTENTS

THREE COINS IN THE BIRDBATH

THE RIDDLE OF THE FIJIS

This all happened, if it happened at all, in the early 1960s. I'm not quite sure which year it was. Maybe it was two years, or three. My time machine is wobbly. Maybe it was only yesterday.

That year we lived, as we do now, in a GI house on a hill called, vaingloriously, if you ask me, Mount Washington. It's a rundown hill in Highland Park, one of the old sections of Los Angeles.

Mount Washington is obsolete, some people say. Fifty years ago it was a very smart hill. There was a large white hotel on top, and a funicular railroad ran up and down between the hotel and a small depot at the bottom. Fashionable couples spent weekends at the hotel.

The railroad is long since gone, but now and then boys will kick up one of its concrete footings, or an old scrap of rusted cable. The hotel is still there, although it isn't a hotel any more. It has been taken over by the Self Realization Fellowship, which is, I believe, a cult of Hinduism. If this is true, I must say they are broadminded; in the evenings during the Christmas season they play *Silent Night, Holy Night* and other Christian carols over their outdoor loudspeaker and the sound flows down over the hill and fills everyone momentarily with brotherly love.

You can see the old hotel from our bedroom window. And if you go into the kitchen and look through the window over the sink, you can see the tower of the Los Angeles city hall. It sticks up over the

roof of our garage. And in summer evenings you can see the lights
of Dodger Stadium on top of the Elysian Park hills, and hear the or-
gan playing *Take Me Out to the Ball Game*.

We have a patio back of the house, and below that a lower yard
we call the second level; and then the land drops away into a deep
and impenetrable canyon, a tangle of wild honeysuckle and sugar-
bush, elderberry, sumac and nightshade, horehound, Scotch broom
and sagebrush. It isn't really impenetrable, I suppose, if you don't
mind groping through poison oak and bumping head-on into red fox,
raccoon, possum, tarantula, skunk, and gopher snake.

Our back yard is unadorned except for the birdbath. I've always
dreamed of owning a marble statue or a fountain. But all we have so
far is the birdbath. It's an unlovely thing; a concrete bowl on a fluted
concrete post. But the birds like it. And sometimes at dusk in the
summer I put *The Fountains of Rome* on the phonograph and look
dimly at the birdbath in the fading gold light and I can easily imagine
it is some undiscovered masterwork of the great Bernini himself.

We have lived here a decade or so—since our younger son Douglas
started going to kindergarten, and his brother Curt to second grade,
at the old Mount Washington elementary school on top of the hill.
Our house is one size too small, like a boy's coat. But we have all got
on well, considering that in some ways we are centuries apart in chemistry and disposition.

I'm an eighteenth-century man myself. I am not sure the human
race has added much to its estate since the steamboat, the Declara-
tion of Independence, and Mozart's serenades, especially *Eine kleine
Nachtmusik*. I own two cars, at last count; an electric toothbrush, a
doorbell, a television set, a power lawnmower, and a telephone with
two extensions. I'd trade them all for an afternoon with Dr. Johnson
in a London pub, on a rainy day.

My wife, on the other hand, is of the nineteenth century. She is
eternally up and about with her rake and shovel and her butcher
knife, her homemade hats and meetings, her mousetraps and poisons,
her scissors and mail-order books and her dressmaker's dummy. She
is plainly of that vigorous century in which the frontiersmen pushed
back the American wilderness and the indefatigable British subdued
the wog, the Fuzzy-Wuzzy, and the whirling dervish.

Our offspring, I'm afraid, are of their own time, although the younger has lately become afflicted with Thoreau. They are in tune with the song of the internal combustion engine and the electric icebox, and appear to be not at all unnerved by the possibility that we shall all be reduced to cinder in the nuclear holocaust.

Dr. René Dubos, the scientist-humanist, says the greatest danger to man is not that he will fail to adapt to the stresses of modern life, and thus become insane, but that he will *succeed* in adapting, and thus lose the very qualities that make us human.

If Dr. Dubos is right, I may represent the hope of the human race. I haven't even adapted, for example, to that inescapable ritual of our culture, the cocktail party. I am unable to hold a *canapé,* a *serviette,* an *apéritif* and a conversation while striking a match and lighting a cigarette for a woman whose name I can't remember. I haven't even learned how to *breathe* at a cocktail party.

If man ever does adapt to the cocktail party he will be a sorry creature indeed, with at least three arms and only one leg, which is all he needs to stand for hours like a stork; lungs that function only on exhaled tobacco smoke, and a diet of limp crackers, fat goose livers, anchovies, and sturgeon eggs.

Another modern institution I haven't adapted to is the Italian movie. I go out of my mind trying to figure out whether Gina, for example, is talking in Italian, and English is being dubbed in, or she's talking in English and the picture is out of synchronization with the sound.

I was watching her lips one night when she said what sounded like, in English, "Ah Vittorio, my turnip, you are a dull husband, but I love you." But it seemed to me, from reading her lips, that she was actually saying, "Why don't you ever wear a shirt, Arnold, and get a job, so we can have a motor scooter like the Giancarlos."

I also haven't adapted to talking elevators, especially those in which an invisible voice commands, "Get back, you—you're standing in the doorway!"

I keep thinking that if an invisible voice can command people to get out of a doorway, and we obey, what commands can't we ultimately be conditioned to obey?

It's hard for an eighteenth-century man to identify in the twentieth

century. I've thought of belonging to something, some fresh, vital
movement in the world, but it never works out.

In college I had a chance to join the Communists, and they certainly
turned out big. But the people who talked to me about it in those
days either talked so low you couldn't hear what they were saying or
yelled in your ear and didn't clean under their fingernails.

One of my troubles is that everything worth belonging to floats
away from me or blows up in my face. It's like a man trying to catch
balloons in a wind.

Years ago, right after the war, I was an angry young man. But the
angry young men had no status then, as a group. They couldn't make
anybody feel guilty. Whenever I got angry and shouted around, people told me to shut up or go back where I came from. I was already
there.

Now the angry young men are selling books and plays and getting
their photographs in newspapers and picture magazines. It might be
a good time to join up, but I'm not angry any more. I found out it
was only a thiamin mononitrate deficiency. I take vitamins for it.

I've considered yoga. But I know a man who took it up one night
at a party and got into one of those positions they get into to achieve
peace of mind and broke his leg in two places getting out of it. He isn't
bitter; just disillusioned.

Existentialism might have been my cup of tea, but those Frenchmen
who seem to think they invented it are quarreling among themselves
and now one can't tell an existentialist from a Zen Buddhist, an angry young man or a television comic.

I've always thought I might have fit into the Lost Generation—
Miss Gertrude Stein's *Génération Perdue*—but I came along too late.
I tried to get in. I lost myself, but nobody ever found me. I read Edna
St. Vincent Millay and burned my candle at both ends. By the time
I got both ends lit, though, it was no longer fashionable, and there
I was, burning away in the wrong generation. Scott Fitzgerald was
dead and Hemingway and the rest of the gang were making money
like a Florida mortician.

Like most men who are never going there, I sometimes dream of
getting away to the South Seas. The very man who panics when he
can't find the can opener may easily fancy himself washed ashore on

a green atoll, the only survivor of some disaster of the deep, building a castle of lotus petals with his bare hands, assisted only by his faithful Fru Fru.

I don't believe that the moon, with all its mysteries, will ever displace the South Seas as the never-never land of the man with his foot caught in the machine age. The oceanic paradise has been slandered by a generation of young Americans who were thrust unwilling on its shores in World War II. Alas, they tasted only the bitter fruit.

I saw those isles when the world was innocent.

I remember Pago Pago. Our ship rushed through dark lava gates and into the harbor. The natives came out to meet us in canoes. The young women swam out to the white ship, supple and brown and buxom, lying on their backs in the green water, with orchids in their ears, plucking homemade lutes and singing liquid songs.

We went ashore in small boats. Everything smelled of coconut and flowers. Everyone laughed. It rained. I walked down a red dirt road in the rain and came upon the small green hotel in which, it is said, Somerset Maugham found his Miss Sadie Thompson. I walked on through wild gardens to villages of palm leaf huts where people lived in innocence of shoes and massive retaliation.

I remember Suva, the jewel of the Fijis. I was among the first ashore. None felt more cosmopolitan than I, sauntering along the sultry streets. These misty islands would be my home. I saw myself in a Conrad novel. Sunburned, grizzled, sinewy, wise. A man who had seen much, who smelled of copra and gin, but told no tales. Yes, from Brisbane to Bangkok, men would speak of me softly as "Smith, the riddle of the Fijis."

I ventured into the white hotel and looked about in the salon and bar for anyone I might have met, perhaps at Claridge's or Shepheard's, in the pages of Maugham and Kipling. I strolled into the perfumed interior of a bric-a-brac shop and negotiated quietly with a fair English girl, fresh out from Wimbledon, for a fiery opal that was quite beyond my means. The girl was pale and exquisite, untouched by tropic sun and rot.

Long after the ship's warning whistle, I ran back to the dock. The gangway had already been hauled aboard. I had to jump for it. I raced below and hopped into my galley whites and dashed to the scullery.

"You alla time late," said the Chinese cook who oversaw my labors. "You alla time dream. Sometime you miss ship. You go native."

The southern seas are as full of islands as the sky of stars. I know of one that is still unspoiled. All I need is a sturdy boat and a fair wind.

I've been saving to buy the boat for years. But something has always come up. The car and the house and the electric range; the hi-fi set, the electric icebox, the shoes, Dr. Pragmire, the dentist; gas for the house in winter; the encyclopedia and the electric drill, the deep freeze, TV, the liability insurance, and the cat.

Now the end is in sight. Soon I can put everything in the boat. All that stands in the way is the automatic sprinkling system for the second level; the humidifier (the house gets dry in winter); the roof and the ophthalmologist. Then we'll be ready to sail, as soon as the boys are out of college.

The hardest part has been getting Fru Fru to plan ahead. I've suggested that she go barefooted around the yard to toughen her feet. She says it would only make them bigger.

"That's all to the good," I pointed out. "The bigger they are the better you can swim."

"I don't want to swim," she said. "I get water in my nose."

"Think of it," I said to her only the other day. "Evenings on the veranda, drinking a cool lemon crush, or maybe a gin and tonic, while the day turns to lavender and then to indigo . . ."

"*What!*" she shouted. She was working the vacuum cleaner and we had to make ourselves heard above its loathsome caterwaul.

"At night," I shouted, "the perfume of the frangipani would float in on the trade winds, and we could hear the innocent laughter of the natives at their luau in the village, living life the way Margaret Mead . . ."

She turned off the vacuum. "D'you mind," she said, "if I take the car tonight? It's a PTA board meeting."

Our life these years has been a Möbius strip. It was Curt who first discovered that.

"I've finally figured it out, Pa," he said one morning as we were waiting for the bathroom. "Life is a Möbius strip."

"What do you mean, a Möbius strip?" I asked.

"It's where you take a strip of something—like a ribbon or some Scotch tape—and give it half a twist and then glue it together at the ends."

"I'm not sure I follow you," I said.

"Well," he explained, "you find out that it never ends, and you can't paint it on one side. It doesn't have one side and it doesn't have two sides. We read about it in math."

So the journals and memorabilia collected here are a kind of Möbius strip, without any beginning or end, and incapable of being painted on one side, or both sides, for that matter.

If there is any moral to be extracted from these tales, I hope it would be that man's individuality is indestructible, his spirit inextinguishable, despite the pressures and abrasions and indignities of life in the modern metropolis.

Even in this age of automobiles, freeways, jukeboxes, TV, the computer, nuclear fusion, the population explosion, feminism, juvenile tyranny, and frozen enchiladas a man can survive and emerge the master of his house, the captain of his soul.

On the other hand maybe there isn't any moral.

Maybe this is only a romanticized account of a few effervescent days in the lives of an eighteenth-century man and his earthy and formidable nineteenth-century wife and their middle-twentieth-century children, living together one yeasty and enchanting year, not long ago.

HOW TO BUILD A CABIN CRUISER

The day was like Liebfraumilch, slightly chilled. I went outdoors to taste it.

A turtledove was chortling in the pine tree. I recognized his voice from last year, but he sounded older, and disenchanted. I wondered if he had gone south for the winter with some flibbertigibbet who gave him the old flimflam for a nighthawk.

Adam, the Dalton boy, was out on his patio practicing variations on a theme by John Philip Sousa on his secondhand trumpet.

The crabgrass, sickly all winter, was suddenly luxuriant as a Persian's beard. I told the boys to mow it. The power mower snarled and spat at them as they tried to prod it awake from its winter hibernation. Then it sulked in silence.

My wife was down on the lower level picking at the earth with a hoe. I lay down under the pepper tree to watch and read some poetry while she worked. She reminded me of Edwin Markham's poignant masterpiece.

"Listen to this," I said. I started reading aloud.

> *Bowed by the weight of centuries she leans*
> *Upon her hoe and gazes on the ground,*
> *The emptiness of ages in her face.*

She leaned on her hoe, gazing at me.

"Get this one," I said:

Spring, the sweet spring, is the year's pleasant king
Then blooms each thing, then maids dance in a ring
Cold doth not sting, the pretty birds do sing
Cuckoo, jug-jug, pu-we, to-witta-woo.

Suddenly she started swinging the hoe wildly about. I rolled over and scrambled to my feet.

"No need to get violent," I said, backing off.

"It was that blasted gopher!" she said. "He stuck his head out. I think I nicked him."

Women revert quickly to the primitive state in the spring when their tulip beds are endangered.

I decided I had bathed enough in sunlight and poetry for one spring day. I went back inside. Then I got the idea of recording bird calls. I plugged in the tape recorder and took the microphone out to the patio. I thought it would be pleasant to listen to the birds of spring some long cold night in deepest winter.

Just as the dove began his plaintive gurgling again the boys got the mower going. Its hideous coughing shattered the limpid air. The dove fell silent and flew away.

"Quiet!" I yelled. "I'm recording the birds!"

They shut off the engine. It was too late. Suddenly it was so quiet I thought I could hear the butterflies chewing lily pistils.

"There he is again!" my wife shrieked from the lower level. *"Help,* somebody!"

"As soon as you finish mowing the lawn," I told the boys, "go see what your mother wants."

I went indoors and took a nap. Spring makes me sleepy.

Spring galvanizes my wife into phenomenal feats of energy. It brings out the best and the worst in her. She can make anything grow. She is especially good at growing mold in the icebox. But she has no sense of the proper place to plant anything.

Other civilized people cut back their jungles. She's growing one. Every morning when I go out on the patio to take a look around, my view is impeded by some new plant she has conjured overnight from the soil.

Nothing she puts in the ground is delicate. If she so much as spits out a watermelon seed, in three months we have a Matto Grosso.

We have a palm tree which is what I believe is called a volunteer. In other words, nobody wanted it. It just sprang up one day, right next to a sidewalk I had built, with exquisite skill, out of concrete. This palm tree pretended, for a few months, to be sickly, so that we all babied it.

Then all of a sudden it put on weight and height like a teen-age boy and turned delinquent. Now you can't walk over my sidewalk without taking a great risk of getting stuck in the eye by one of its malignant fronds, and its greedy roots are beginning to buckle the walk.

Everything she gave to the earth that spring had to be taken back later and put someplace else. She planted a Brazilian palm tree once by the back door of the garage. It sprang up like a missile. One couldn't open the door.

"I thought it was a miniature," she explained.

Nothing she grew was a miniature. If she planted a violet it would turn out to be a man-eating orchid. Once she planted what she called an "ornamental shrub" in front of what I like to call the servant's entrance. Actually it's only the back door. The only servant we have is the milkman.

This ornamental shrub turned out to have a zest for life that was horrifying. It thrust thick arms into the sky and crawled over the ground like a crocodile. Finally the day came when the milkman couldn't get in through the servant's entrance. He had to leave the milk outside in the sun. This, I understand, destroys the vitamin D. I had to buy an ax and hack a passage through her loathsome ornament so the family could have good bones.

On weekends she descended into the canyon with her rake and machete to extend her wilderness, laboring with missionary zeal. She would vanish from view for hours on end. We couldn't even see her from the patio, but we always knew where she was because a cloud of birds formed over her position. She turned up a lot of worms.

In the grip of these passions she wouldn't even come back to the house to cook. Now and then I sent a boy down with water. We had to make our own sandwiches and answer the doorbell while she was down there grappling with the stony earth under the birds.

Sometimes one of the dogs went down to see her and came back an hour or so later, panting with thirst and fatigue. I thought of pinning notes to their collars, so we could at least communicate.

Meanwhile, everything in the house went to pieces. It was like the old French Empire. We kept extending our frontiers while the core decayed. I couldn't get her to read history so she'd realize what was happening to us.

One April morning she clomped into the house in her muddy shoes and asked me to come outside and help her.

"I want to plant a peach tree," she explained.

I was in the den reading *How to Build a Cabin Cruiser*. My heart was at sea. I was in no mood to grapple with the earth.

"Ever since I was a little girl," she said, "I've wanted my own peach tree."

An approach like that is hard to fend off. I put down *How to Build a Cabin Cruiser* and went outside with her.

"There," she said, pointing out a spot in the canyon below the second level. A tree already stood there, a stubborn-looking tree with multiple trunks, thorny limbs and little yellow flowers.

"There is already a tree there," I pointed out.

She said it would have to come out. It was not a peach tree.

"What kind of a tree is it?" I asked.

"*Parkinsonia aculeata,*" she said. She always amazes me with her knowledge of nature's nomenclature. "It will have to come out."

I walked around the *Parkinsonia aculeata,* like a wrestler sizing up his foe. It was only six feet tall or so, and scrawny looking, but somehow tough, like an Apache brave. I got a shovel and took my shirt off and made a move at it. I leaped back screaming.

"It has thorns," my wife said.

I looked at my hands and arms. Beads of blood oozed from a dozen tiny wounds. I went into the house and put on a denim jacket and got the saw and crawled under the thing and sawed through the trunks. They were hard as baseball bats.

The tree started to fall. I tried to crawl clear, but too late. It caught me. I screamed.

"You ought to wear gloves," my wife said.

"It isn't my hands," I said, "that I'm worried about."

I put on gloves and gingerly dragged the dismembered thing clear and started digging around the stump. I dug, and the sun crawled across the sky. I dug some more.

Three feet down the root was still as big as a man's leg and cross-roots reached out like brawny arms. I got a grip and yanked on the stump. Nothing gave.

Across the canyon I saw Dalton sitting on his patio. He was drinking beer and watching through his spyglass.

I went out and got the long dog chain and looped it around the root and went downhill a ways and gave it a pull.

"What are you doing?" she asked.

"I'm using my head," I explained.

I yanked it again and the chain snapped. It struck like a rattlesnake. I ducked. It caught me on the left ear.

Sometimes when I'm bruised and frustrated I take refuge in books. I went inside and got a cold beer and buried myself in *Bartlett's Familiar Quotations*. She followed me inside and got a grape juice.

"You resting?" she asked.

"I'm thinking," I said.

I read a while.

" 'Nature,' " I read aloud, " 'is immovable.' Euripides."

"It's only a little old stump," she said.

" 'Drive out nature with a pitchfork' " I read, " 'and she will always come back.' Horace."

"What do they know about *Parkinsonia aculeatas?*" she scoffed.

"Euripides and Horace," I explained, "were very wise men."

"Agh," she said. She went outside.

I got the Garden Book and looked up *Parkinsonia aculeata*. "Ugly thorns, sparse foliage," it said. It didn't say how to get one out of the ground.

When I went outside again she was planting the peach tree. The *Parkinsonia aculeata* was stretched out dead on the ground like a slain dragon.

She smiled up at me. "I just dug a little more and gave it a tug."

I went back in the house and got two cans of cold beer and went over to Dalton's.

Later that spring she had an even greater triumph. It was the *Tigridia pavonia*. It happened one Sunday afternoon. There are sudden moments on a Sunday afternoon, when the curtains are drawn against the sun and the house is cool and still, that seem to float in time.

I was floating along in one of these silver bubbles one such Sunday when there was a rattling at the patio doors and she stuck her head in.

"I can't come in," she said. "I'm all muddy."

She was wearing a blue seersucker sunsuit. Her shoes and knees and hands were muddy.

"Why can't you look like Lana Turner or Ava Gardner," I asked, "in those jungle movies, with only a little smudge on your cheek? Why do you always have to get your knees muddy?"

"Are you terribly busy?" she said. "I want you to come look at something. There isn't much time."

Actually, I was reading a magazine article on how to re-string a tennis racket. But there was an urgency in her voice that made me get up and follow her.

"It's something you have to see for yourself," she said as she led me across the yard and got down on her hands and knees and looked intensely at something. I got down beside her.

"What is it, for God's sake?" I demanded. I was afraid it was something I would have to kill.

"*Tigridia pavonia*," she whispered. "Isn't it marvelous?"

"*Tigridia pavonia*? What's that?"

"They call it the Mexican tiger flower."

It was a cream-colored, cup-shaped bloom with an interior of dark lavender leopard spots.

"Well, I suppose it's pretty enough," I admitted. "But why the all-fired hurry?"

"They only last a day," she said softly. "Look at it. It makes all my feeble efforts worth while. All the years. Remember when we were first married and I got all those sweet pea seeds at Montgomery Ward and planted them along the fence? And they didn't grow?"

"No," I said. "I don't remember."

"I guess I never told you. I was so ashamed. Sweet peas are the easiest of all things to grow."

"So what," I said. "I imagine the Lord thought you were lucky enough getting me for a husband, you didn't need sweet peas."

"It's taken all these years," she said, "to get this flower, and to-morrow it will be gone."

I went back in the house and tried to read. But I had lost interest in how to re-string a tennis racket.

I kept thinking about beauty that only lasts a day.

DALTON

Sunday afternoons at the Daltons are meat and drink for the soul. They're an exciting mixture of culture and nature in the raw. I often feel like the late Ernest Hemingway.

The Daltons live across the canyon from us in an old red frame three-story house with the lines of a tramp freighter. They have a swimming pool, which is the center of our social, intellectual, and physical life. Dalton is a professor of something at the University of Southern California. Mythology, I believe. He's never actually said. Dalton stays home a lot when the weather is good. He says he stays home to read and theorize. He also cleans the pool. The algae drive him ape.

Dalton likes to sit on the pool deck in an old canvas chair, watching the wild life of the hill, including us, through his spyglass. In his youth Dalton set out to sail around the world in a ketch, but he never made it. The ketch foundered on the rocks off Baja California and was lost. All he saved was the spyglass.

Dalton has grown mild in middle age. He likes to have younger students about. He holds court in his swimming trunks, drinking vodka gimlets and talking about his life or mythology. He is said to have been a formidable hunter in his bachelor days, as well as a linguist, and occasionally, when something wild ventures up from the bush of the canyon, a visitor at the Dalton place may be treated to a momentary flash of his old nerve and cunning.

We once saw him deal with a snake and a gopher on a single Sunday afternoon.

I remember how the day began. I had awakened early and got up to make a cup of instant coffee. The clock on the electric range said ten-thirty.

A brassy lament came drifting across the canyon, like a bugle call in one of those old movies about the French Foreign Legion. It was young Adam Dalton, I realized, practicing on his trumpet. The tune was familiar, but I couldn't place it.

After he finished, the theme kept running through my mind. I knew it would trouble me all day. He started up again. I woke my wife.

"Hear that trumpet?" I said.

She listened. "Yes," she said. "It's Adam."

"I know. But what's he playing? Taps?"

"Of course not. It's *Happy Birthday to You*. It's your birthday. Remember?"

"Good Lord!" I groaned. "So it is." It had slipped my mind.

I went out on the patio to acknowledge the salute. The trumpet stopped. Band music came crashing over the canyon. Dalton had hooked their phonograph to the loudspeaker by the pool. They were playing *The Marine Corps Hymn*.

The phone rang. It was Dalton.

"You hear that, Jack?" he said. "We're playing *your* song, for your birthday. It's *The Halls of Montezuma*."

"Turn it off!" I told him. "You'll get me in trouble. It's not *my* song. I was only in the Reserves."

He invited us over for a birthday party. "Ilya Ransome's brought her ham," he said.

The Ransomes had just moved into the old Capone place on the hill. We called it the Capone place because the man who lived in it before the Ransomes took it was mixed up in the rackets and had been hauled off to prison. Mrs. Ransome had recently baked a big ham, but that same day Ransome had been sent out of town on business. She had been driving the ham everywhere she went, in her little Fiat, trying to get people to help eat it.

We hurried over. Young Adam blew *Happy Birthday* again and they gave me three books as presents: *Beverly of Graustark,* by

George Barr McCutcheon; *Just Folks,* by Edgar A. Guest; and
Exposition Memories—San Diego, 1916.

"Just what I wanted," I said. "I've been looking for these for over
forty years. Where'd you find them?"

"Ilya found them in the garage," said Mrs. Dalton, "when she
moved into the old Capone place."

I found a pressed geranium in *Just Folks.*

"Just think," I said. "This desiccated, fragile thing is as old as I
am."

Everyone fell into a thoughtful silence.

Later, one of Dalton's friends from the university came by with
his guitar and sang folk songs. It may have been the music that at-
tracted the snake. Or maybe the gopher. We don't know.

The snake had been visiting the Daltons all spring. Dalton kept
chasing him away, but he always came back. Dalton thought he
was drawn by the shade, or by Mrs. Dalton's cooking, which is old
world and aromatic.

Dalton liked the snake. He has a tolerant attitude toward all living
things. Besides, he observed, it was probably only a gopher snake,
friendly and harmless, and maybe lonely. Mrs. Dalton's reaction was
entirely irrational. Whenever she saw the snake she turned catatonic.

He came back that Sunday just after I surfaced from skin diving.
I love it down there in what Cousteau calls the silent world, although
there isn't much to see in Dalton's pool but algae.

Dalton's colleague was plucking his guitar and singing a folk lament
about a hard rock miner whose only love was the ore cart mule. Dalton was mixing a gimlet. Mrs. Dalton had gone into the house for
more anchovies. In a moment she appeared in the doorway, white
and popeyed. She looked like a halibut I saw once that had just been
pulled out of the bay at Ensenada.

"He's back!" Mrs. Dalton shrieked. Then she went catatonic.

We men trooped through the house and into the shady little garden
by the kitchen. The snake was curled up under a tree. He was beige
with brown rosettes. He had a forked tongue.

"What kind is it?" I cried. "He might be poisonous."

"Don't worry about that, old man," said Dalton. "You'll notice his head isn't pitted. All poisonous snakes in Western America, I believe you'll find, have pits in front of the eyes."

"He might have escaped from a zoo," my wife said.

"Run home," I told one of my boys, "and get the Encyclopaedia Britannica."

"Never mind that," said Dalton. "Get me the rake. I'll just give the bugger a nudge." He was quite cool.

"Bring me Volume Twenty," I said. "I think it's the one from Sarsaparilla to Sorcery. I'll look him up."

Nobody paid me any attention. It's one of my idiosyncrasies. I often have an academic rather than a physical response to situations of peril.

Young Adam got the rake. Dalton jousted with the reptile like Don Quixote jousting with Evil. Dalt's a great one to overplay a role. Finally the snake stuck his tongue out, yawned and slithered away. He slipped through a crack in the wall and vanished down the canyon.

We trooped back through the house. Mrs. Dalton had recovered from her catalepsy.

"Will you men please quit tracking through my kitchen in your wet feet!" she scolded.

We filed out glumly, an abject little crew in our clammy swim trunks. That's the way of life. Man can drive the wild beasts from woman's door, only to be chastised for petty transgressions.

We went back to the pool and the professor with the guitar sang a lament about Adam and Eve and sin.

After exorcising the gopher snake, Dalton and I fell into an intellectual dialogue, which is our custom. On this particular Sunday the conversation somehow had drifted onto courtship techniques among the warm-hearted vertebrates.

"Observation of the chukker partridge," I observed, "has shown that the female often spurns the aggressive male, preferring to share her life with the more refined type bird."

"Where'd you hear that?" Dalton said skeptically.

"It's not the sort of thing one *hears*," I pointed out. "I *read* it."

"Where'd you read it?" he said. Dalton happens to know that, because I read so much, trying to keep up with everything, I can never remember where I read any particular item. He has a mean habit of challenging me to declare my source.

"I believe I read it in my drawer," I said. "I mean I read it somewhere that I cut out. With scissors. It's in my drawer."

His eyes glazed over with doubt. My wife rushed to my aid.

"You read it out loud to me the other night," she said. "Remember? Only you don't have it right. It was the other way. It said the *female* partridge was the aggressive sex. It was in the *Ladies' Home Journal*."

"Don't be naïve," I told her. "It couldn't be the female that's more aggressive. That's only among the higher primates, where females have control of the money."

"All the same," she said, "it was in the *Journal*. Or else *The New Yorker*."

"Speaking of birds," Dalton said, "guess what the only bird is who can climb down a tree head first."

"The bronze grackle?" I guessed.

"Wrong," said Dalton. "The white-breasted nuthatch."

"Where'd you read that?" I asked. I thought he was making it up.

"I didn't read it anywhere," he said. "I saw one *do* it once in Wisconsin."

That's one of Dalton's troubles. He has a tendency to rely on personal experiences, from which he makes enormous generalizations. He doesn't seem to grasp the scientific method very well for a university professor.

We were at this impasse when we were galvanized by a cry that is all too familiar in the western suburbs.

"Gopher!"

The men sprang to their feet. Our young had sighted one of the sinister rodents on the planted slope below the pool deck. He had popped his head out of a hole near Mrs. Dalton's asters.

We ran to the rail and stood there, waiting for the gopher to show his head. He popped out again. He blinked at us and shot back out of sight as if yanked on a string.

"Ugh!" said Mrs. Dalton. "What *is* it?"

"Gopher," said Dalton. "Now you see? If we'd left the gopher snake alone, *he* could get the gopher. This is what we get for fooling with the balance of nature."

"Maybe it's only a squirrel," I suggested. Dalton gave me his Laurence Olivier smile.

"Or a raccoon," my wife said. "They're quite cute."

Mrs. Dalton ran into the house and got the Garden Encyclopedia.

"*Gopher,*" she read. "A small, burrowing, pouched rodent. The western gardener's public enemy number one."

"It's a gopher, all right," my wife said. "I saw the pouches."

"I'll get my slingshot," said young Adam Dalton.

"You wouldn't have a chance," said his father. "I'll make a lethal device."

He got an old rat trap and a string and a stick. We watched the old expert in fascination. He tied one end of the string to the trap and the other to the stick.

"When he springs the trap," Dalton explained, "this stick will keep him from pulling it down in his tunnel. Then we take hold of the stick and *pull him out.*"

"Amazing!" I whispered.

Dalton set the trap, forcing the lethal bar back against the resistance of the spring and fixing the latch.

"Now," he said, "to place the trap over the gopher's hole."

He climbed out over the deck and dropped to the slope and started down. It looked difficult and dangerous.

"Don't tramp on the asters, dear!" shouted Mrs. Dalton.

"Maybe you ought to go with him," said my wife.

"Yes," I agreed. "Maybe I ought. I'll just go along and hold his gimlet."

Dalton put the trap in the mouth of the hole and stuck the stick in the earth.

"Careful, old man," I warned, "you'll lose yourself a finger."

"Don't worry about me," said Dalton. "Done this a thousand times."

He accidentally jerked the string. The trap sprang. Dalton leaped back. He lost his footing and crashed backward into a tangle of bushes.

"Get *up,* darling!" cried Mrs. Dalton. "You're in the poison *ivy!*"

Dalton sat up. The gopher popped out of his hole, blinked and vanished again. Dalton climbed to his feet and stumbled out of the poison ivy. He was muddy. He limped.

"It's that old knee again," he groaned. "Stanford-Cal game—'36. God what a game!"

"There was an awful crowd," recalled Mrs. Dalton. "He hit his knee on the turnstile."

Dalton started to struggle up the slope.

"Don't limp on the *flowers,* love," said Mrs. Dalton.

Dalton reached the deck and sank into a canvas chair. I handed him his gimlet. He looked up gratefully.

"Thanks, old man," he said.

Mrs. Dalton dabbed at his forehead with a wet towel.

"Great white hunter," she murmured.

"Get the bugger tomorrow," Dalton panted. "Use poison gas."

The following Sunday, as I remember, the Daltons had a young lady over who could recite Emily Dickinson by heart. Dalton got stung by a bee and had to be driven to the emergency hospital down the hill. He has an allergy to the bee's venom.

The gopher is still at large. Mrs. Dalton calls it Moby Dick.

YOU'VE GOT SAND IN MY PAJAMAS

I believe a man should keep fit after his days of glory on the playing field are over. I have no patience with the middle-aged slob and his boozy memories of an eighty-yard run.

I began spring training that year on a Sunday morning. The air was sauterne. The yard, I saw, was in glut again. I knew my wife was going to have a real battle. I decided to buy her a new hoe.

I got a rag out of the garage and wiped the rust off the horizontal bar. I had been rather sharp on the bar as a lad. I'd been looking forward to polishing up the old skills ever since the boys had installed the thing in our yard.

I jumped up and caught the bar and was hanging there, letting myself stretch out, when my wife rushed outside.

"What are you doing?" she cried.

"What does it look like I'm doing?" I said. "I'm hanging by my hands from the horizontal bar."

"You'll kill yourself," she prophesied, "with your bad back."

"Just the opposite," I explained. "I'm relaxing my back without actually doing anything strenuous."

"Well at least don't you think you ought to put on something besides your pajamas?"

"Why should I? I'm warm enough. It's bracing."

"I mean," she said, "how it looks. *Outdoors.*"

"What do I care how it looks? If the neighbors don't like it, they don't have to look. It's a well-established legal principle."

She went back inside, shaking her head.

I decided to warm up with a few little-drops. The little-drop is rather elementary. You swing by your knees until, at the peak of a forward swing, you straighten your legs and drop to your feet. I must have done it a million times as a kid.

I got my legs up over the bar and hung by my knees and swung back and forth a few times. I got dizzy. I realized I must be a little weak from the sun. I grabbed hold of the bar with my hands. I couldn't get my legs down off the bar. My knees were stuck.

"Come out!" I shouted. "Help!"

She ran out. "What's the matter! What's the matter!" she shouted.

"Don't just stand there!" I cried. "I've got a cramp or something. I can't let go. Grab me around the shoulders."

She grabbed me around the shoulders. "Now lift up," I told her. She lifted up. My knees loosened. My arms relaxed. I let go. We both fell down in the sand pit.

"Why didn't you hold me up, for God's sake!" I cried. "You nearly killed me."

"I didn't know you were going to let go," she shrieked. "Good heavens, anyway! You crazy man!"

"Now look what you've done," I said. "You've got sand in my pajamas."

"Good," she said. "Now maybe you'll take them off."

"I just might," I threatened. "Speaking of appearances, when are you going to get after this yard? It's a jungle. I feel like Tarzan of the apes."

She looked despairingly over the great green veldt of the yard and the weedy canyon.

"Me Jane," she sighed.

The phone rang. I went inside to answer it. It was Dalton.

"Say," he said, "did you hurt yourself?"

"Hurt myself how?"

"Falling off the horizontal bar. You were hanging from it."

"Yes, I know," I said. "It's all right. It was only an exercise."

"Listen," I asked my wife when she came in. "Is it spring?"

"Of course," she said. "It's been spring for weeks. How did *you* catch on?"

"I figured it out," I explained, "because Dalton's already watching us through his spyglass."

In my determination to keep fit I've tried almost everything, but nothing seems quite suitable. For a while after the war I kept fit with do-it-yourself chores around the house. But most everything challenging in that line has long since been done. There's only a little maintenance work left around the place, of the sort that a woman can easily do, such as plumbing, glazing, and roofing.

I tried tennis. My wife and I bought rackets and went at it exuberantly. Some of the regulars down at the courts said they thought I had a flair for the game. It was said that I rushed the net well, although not always at the proper moment.

I might have gone on with tennis, but I have weak eyes and when I look up into the sky on a sunny day I sneeze. This didn't do my serve any good.

Golf looked like the answer for a time. I love the clothes and trappings and camaraderie of the game and the atmosphere. It lifts the spirit of a deskbound city man to escape to the misty green hills and chase the capricious little ball over the dewy glens and dells in the morning chill.

However, I found that as my game improved I was playing it more and enjoying it less. This was explained to me by a friend. As my play became more nearly flawless, he explained, I would become increasingly tense and irritable. Golf would no longer be a relaxing game. It would become a demon, a burden, a monkey on my back.

"By the time you're playing regularly in the low seventies," he told me, "you'll blow your stack every time you shoot a bogie."

I had to give it up. I'm tense enough already.

I even tried long-distance running once. I had become interested in this lonely discipline through my boys, both of whom are cross-country men, and the great college runner Vic Zwolak, who has spoken eloquently of the loneliness of the long-distance runner.

"All your muscles tighten and hurt," Zwolak says, "and your lungs are fighting for oxygen. You know that nobody, but nobody, can help you . . ."

I wondered if I might achieve that zenith of physical and spiritual exertion and aloneness. Friends and family are a joy. But only in loneliness does a man's spirit burn with a clear blue flame.

I made my first run one evening. My younger son was getting into his blue sweat suit to work out on the hill.

"I'll go on ahead," I told him. "I'm not in top shape."

"You going to run like that?" he asked. "In regular clothes?"

"You think I'm going to run in my underwear?" I said. "People around here already think I'm a kook."

I set off down the hill. Our cross-country course makes a steep, dog-leg descent, past houses, then a big, climbing loop, through wilderness, back to our place. It was dusk. The living rooms of the houses, behind their undraped windows, were softly lit like theater sets.

A dog the size of a bear bounded out from a dark porch. A large wolf joined him, followed by a dachshund. The brutes set to yelping insanely.

A door flew open. A man leaned out. "What is it?" a woman shouted from inside. "I don't know," the man said. "A man running."

Another door flew open. The Gribble boy popped out. "It's Mr. Smith!" he shrieked. He ran after me.

I decided to walk past the houses, to avoid further hysteria, and to run only in the wilderness.

When I passed the last house the sky had darkened. The road was shadowy. I started running. My shoes rang like gunshots on the pavement. My pulse began to race. I grew quite sure that someone was following me. I ran faster.

All my muscles tightened and hurt. My lungs fought for oxygen. I knew that nobody, but nobody, could help me.

My son passed me like a blue wraith, running smoothly.

"Take it easy, Pa," he called out. He flew on out of sight.

I stopped to rest. I walked back down the road and up the hill past the houses. Life—the eternal play—was in full progress on the glowing sets behind the picture windows. In one scene a housewife in a red dress was serving dinner. The Gribble boy was watching a cartoon on TV. The man who had shouted was reading the funnies and drinking a beer.

I climbed back up the hill to our house. A little loneliness goes a long way.

Not long after that experience I tried walking. I walked about two miles the first day, which was perhaps overdoing it for a start, and also I made the error of setting off downhill, instead of up. By the time I got to the corner, I was too tired to start back up the hill. I had to rest a while at the P-M Cafe.

As I was walking home, a police car passed me, going slow. I could see the policeman scrutinizing me with his peripheral vision. I'm told they have to have excellent peripheral vision to get on the force. He drove on a way and made a U-turn, making another pass at me.

Suddenly I remembered I didn't have my wallet. I was seized with apprehension. What if he stopped to question me? I couldn't prove who I was. I would be arrested as a vagrant. I wouldn't know what to say. It had been years since I'd been out walking alone. How could I explain not being in a car?

The policeman drove on and vanished around a corner. I hurried on up the hill. It had been a narrow escape.

The Daltons were coming down the hill in their old Studebaker. Mrs. Dalton was driving, which has always struck me as incongruous, if you know her. They stopped.

"Where you going?" Dalton called.

"Nowhere," I said. "Just taking a walk."

"Is anything wrong?"

"I don't think so," I said. I decided it was just as well not to tell them about almost getting arrested.

"Well, can we give you a lift?" he said.

"No," I said. "I'll just walk on. I'm really not going anywhere."

They nudged on down the hill, the way she drives. I walked back home.

"How'd the walk go?" my wife said.

"Not so good," I admitted.

"What's the matter? Too much too soon?"

"Nothing wrong with me," I said. "It's just that you can't take a walk any more. They either want to arrest you or give you a ride."

Later I put my faith in *Adult Physical Fitness,* a book put out by the President's Council of Physical Fitness.

"If you have decided that it is time to get in shape," says the introduction, "you have a rewarding adventure ahead."

The booklet offers a program of exercises by which the average flabby American can recapture the taut belly and elastic limbs of youth.

The program begins with a group of orientation exercises. You do these for a week to get in good enough shape to start the real program.

The orientation is a breeze. The first night I ran through the bend-and-stretch, the knee lift, the wing stretcher and the half-knee bend without mishap.

"The old musculo-skeletal machine is still pretty smooth," I observed to my wife and younger son. They had been looking on with morbid fascination, as if expecting something within me to snap.

While I was doing the prone arch something struck them funny. In the prone arch you lie on your stomach, with your hands under your thighs, and raise your head, shoulders, and legs in the air. As one does this, the air is forced suddenly from the lungs, causing one to emit a barking sound. Something like "aurk!"

I lay on my stomach and raised my head and shoulders and legs. "Aurk!" I said.

My son got out of his chair and staggered across the room with his hands to his stomach, like a man who has been shot on *Gunsmoke.* He leaned against the wall, wheezing and pounding it. He looked like a man possessed.

"What's the matter with him?" I asked, rolling over and sitting up.

My wife was lying prone on the couch. Her head was in a pillow. She seemed to have the hiccoughs.

"What's the matter with her?" I asked.

"A *seal,* Pa!" the boy blubbered. "That's what you looked like! A *seal!*"

"You mean a sea lion," I said. "Not a seal. Seals have pointed ears."

Or is it the other way around?

I left them to their childish hysteria and went out on the front porch to do the ankle stretch. You need a step for the ankle stretch. You stand with the balls of your feet on the step and stretch your arms out in front, as if preparing to do a swan dive, and raise and lower your heels, up and down.

I was doing the ankle stretch when Mrs. Gribble turned up our walk. She was collecting for something.

"Good Lord! Mr. Smith," she cried. "Is something wrong?"

"No," I said. "I'm stretching my ankles."

"Oh," she said.

"Do you think I look like a seal?"

"Why, no," she said.

Sometimes I think I'm living in the same house with odd folk.

I stayed with the President's program for a week, but the only result was that I caught a cold, probably from lying on the floor in my underwear for the prone arch.

Ironically, the discipline in which I had the greatest faith brought me only agony and humiliation.

This was isometric contraction. I first learned about isometric contraction in a magazine. It is a form of exercise in which one doesn't have to move a muscle. One simply places his palms against a wall, for example, and pushes for ten seconds. Isometric contraction strengthens and tones the muscles through *resistance*. There is no need to run or lift, or strike or bat anything, or anybody.

Scientists learned about isometric contraction by tying down one leg of a frog. The frog kept pulling this leg, trying to get free, and the tied leg grew stronger than the free leg, which the frog kept exercising by waving it around foolishly, like a tennis racket.

Besides pushing a wall to tone up the back and arms, one should suck in the stomach for ten seconds as near to the backbone as it will go. In one month this is supposed to produce a strong neck and trim two inches off the waist.

I worked out a little routine. Every morning when I got up I'd go into the bathroom and shut the door. Then I pushed against the door as hard as I could for ten seconds. This not only toned up my arms and back, but also kept anybody else from getting in the bathroom for at least ten seconds, which was a better head start than I usually have.

At first I used the living room instead of the bathroom for my morning push. This was all right, but when I tried sucking in my stomach as near to my backbone as it would go, my pajama bottoms fell down. This is an embarrassing position to be caught in when you are holding up a wall.

Isometric contraction worked fine for a week. But then I developed a side effect. I was flat on my back for two days. I was pushing the wall as usual one morning when something in my lower vertebral regions went twang, like a well-plucked banjo string. I fell to my knees and screamed.

I couldn't stand up. Through sheer courage and a fierce contempt for pain I got myself to bed. We put the heating pad under my back and turned up the electric blanket. Wrapped in this cocoon of warmth, I found that the pain would subside if I lay absolutely still.

I also had the druzzles at the time, though, and now and then I had to sneeze. Whenever I sneezed, my body jerked. Then I screamed. The scream followed closely on my normal sneeze, which sounds something like *"Who is she?"*

So when I sneezed, it sounded like *"Who is she? Yii!"*

This performance invariably threw my loved ones into a frenzy of hysterical laughter. They staggered about, hugging themselves, their faces twisted into caricatures of sadistic ecstasy.

On the second day, when they thought I was getting better, they went away and left me. Limp with pain, I was sinking into oblivion when the doorbell rang. I sat up. This made me scream. The doorbell stopped ringing. Then it began again.

By rolling over gently I reached the edge of the bed. I lowered myself to the floor on my hands and knees. I crawled into the living room in my pajamas. I reached up and opened the door.

It was Mrs. Treble. She gaped down at me and staggered back. "Good heavens, Mr. Smith!" she gasped. "Is something *wrong?*"

"No," I said, "I'm just looking for a cuff link."

"I thought I heard something scream," she said.

"It must have been the TV," I said. Just then I sneezed.

"Who is she? Yii!" I screamed.

Mrs. Treble turned white. She stumbled down the sidewalk and ran for her car.

By the end of that miserable week I could get up on my feet. I couldn't stand up straight, but I could take little crouching steps. Everybody said I looked like a chimpanzee, but not as smart.

When I was able to get on my feet and into a car I went to Dr. Rue, the osteopath. A man's back is like a piano. He shouldn't try to tune it himself.

My wife drove me to the doctor's office. I shouldn't have, but I opened the garage door so she could get the car out. It gave up an agonized creak.

"I thought I told the boys to oil that thing," I said.

"They did," my wife said. "That was probably your back."

A woman who can go for years without cracking a joke always seems to develop a sense of humor when her husband is in pain. I don't know why that is.

The doctor didn't laugh. He took me into a little office and asked for the history of my trouble. He poised a pen over my data card.

"Well," I said, with a bitter little laugh, "it's quite a long story."

I told him about the war, when I fell out of the second-story window, and about the time I hurt my back shaving and about how I had now unsprung something while pushing against the living-room wall.

His eyebrows went up the slightest bit, about an eighth of an inch.

"I was practicing isometric contraction," I explained. "It's a form of exercise you can do without moving any muscles."

He nodded and wrote something on my card. Doctors get used to all kinds, I guess.

"Well, take off your coat, shirt, and trousers," he said. "Let's take a look at you."

When I was ready, he came back in and took a look. It was my sacroiliac.

"Lie down," he said, "on your back."

I lay down on my back. He took hold of my left foot and gave my leg an outward crank, the way you wind a clock. He cranked my right leg in.

"The trouble is," he explained, "that man was not intended to walk upright. Adam and Eve didn't sin when they ate that apple. They sinned when they reached up for it with one hand."

He took my right knee and doubled my right leg back. He moved the knee around, like shifting gears on a sports car, then moved suddenly into third, a maneuver which put my right kneecap under my chin.

"How did that feel?" he asked.

"It felt," I explained, "like when the waiter takes a knife and fork and lifts the entire backbone out of a broiled trout. That is, it felt like I was the trout."

He nodded. "Right."

He took my head in both hands and gave it a bit of a spin, like a man hefting a bowling ball. It sounded like one of those ratchet toys kids drive adults out of their minds with.

"You ever break anybody's neck that way?" I gasped.

He stifled an insane chuckle. "Not for several weeks," he said.

He cranked up my arms and told me to get dressed.

"For the next few days," he said, "don't make any sudden moves. Don't reach for anything."

"What about," I asked, "lifting the garage door?"

"Better not," he said. "That's like Adam reaching for the apple."

"What did he say?" my wife asked on the way home.

"He said," I told her, "to let you open the garage door from now on."

THEORIES OF THE NEW LEISURE CLASS

The teen years are often said to be a rude and painful experience, like falling downstairs in the dark. I wouldn't care to go through them again if only because I never liked dancing in a gymnasium.

Our teen-agers, according to statistics, are afloat on a rosy stream of plenty. They spend ten billion dollars a year for such creature comforts as lipstick, electric razors, phonograph records, surfboards, sports cars, TV sets, and ice cream.

This new buying power reflects our general productivity and prosperity, and nobody can despise good times. Besides, it is human to want to make our young happy and see that they have things we didn't have, such as private telephones.

I was a teen-ager before the portable radio. I spent many an hour on the beach reading *Whiz Bang* magazine when I might have been listening to Rudy Vallee. A man who has suffered like that can hardly deny his own offspring a transistor set or two.

It is a harsh irony that just as he sinks into the mellow seas of early middle age a man has to come to grips with the early teen-age mind.

In my attempt to make contact with this generation I agreed one evening to take part in a panel discussion of life in general with a number of these young primitives.

I learned a few things. The trouble with the younger teen-agers is that their parents ask too many nosy questions, don't understand life and have a tendency to keep the telephone tied up.

About the telephone. This instrument is vital to the social development of the junior-grade teen-ager. Especially the female. It is the means of exchanging current data on the world of fashion, the arts (motion pictures and TV), and boys.

If parents need the momentary use of the telephone in the critical period between five o'clock and midnight, they should state the nature of the emergency and then be brief.

Television. Surprisingly, this hypnotic device does not have so powerful a hold over our younger teen-agers as you might suppose. In the struggle for young minds it is losing ground to books. Good, hard-hitting comic books. In many families the parents now are permitted to turn TV on and off as they choose.

Going steady. This is too large and flexible a concept for the adult mind. In the first place, going steady doesn't mean going steady.

Going steady, as I now understand it, is an agreement between a male and a female of the group to "go around" on an almost constant basis. That is, neither goes around with another boy or girl almost.

People who are going steady happen to prefer each other to anybody else, at the moment. They have sworn fidelity until they become more interested in two other people.

It really is no more tenuous an association than many on which great enterprises are undertaken, such as international treaties. The understanding may be tacit, and is tacitly licit, we hope.

As an institution it is similar to marriage in Hollywood, although more binding.

Going steady does not mean the same thing in junior high as in senior high. In senior high it means a social contract has been entered into that might reasonably be expected to culminate in marriage or, as one young authority put it, "anything."

In junior high going steady is not invested with such cataclysmic potential. It is an end in itself, like reading a comic book. It won't get you anywhere but it helps pass the time while you are aging.

As one of the other fathers on the panel said, "Well, heck! If that's all going steady means, why, I think girls should go steady with as many boys as they want to."

Of course, that father has only a son.

To make any significant penetration of the early teen-age mind a man has to get out of the house and study them at their rites. The most important of these, I learned, is the regular Friday night bacchanal at the neighborhood movie theater.

These are the shrines to which the little scholars make pilgrimage after they have been paroled for the weekend by the educational institutions.

On a Friday night the neighborhood movie house is a weird arena. If you get caught in one innocently, as I did, you will think you are playing Rugby in a dark ice-cream parlor.

I stumbled into one of these rumbles one night, and for a week my stomach was knotted up like a schoolboy's shoelaces. So far as I could see when the lights went up for a popcorn break, my wife and I were almost the only fool adults in the house.

There were a man and woman way in the back, but I believe they were with the FBI. I hope so.

Awash in that swarm of squealing juveniles, I felt like a square old log, tossed on an adolescent sea.

When we sat down a boy in front of me who had eyes and a neck like an owl swiveled around and stared at us. He was eating an Abba Zaba and slopping it down with something out of a paper cup.

I tried to appear nonchalant under this unnerving scrutiny. I rested the back of my head against the shoe of the lad behind me and concentrated on the movie.

It was a flimsy little comedy of sex in the suburbs, full of juicy *contretemps* and salted with *double entendre* and innuendo that even we square adults could dig.

When one of the slick females in the movie got off one of these sly shafts the urchin at my left would gulp his popcorn down and holler "Woo hoo hoo!" in a most lascivious way. I studied the little lecher and figured him for ten, going on eleven.

The movie was secondary to the social aspects of the evening, however. The major activities seemed to be eating, drinking, musical chairs, track and field events in the aisles, conversation, community laughing, and a re-enactment of the War between the Sexes at junior high school level.

Some girls two rows ahead of us were wearing black and red leotards. They scrunched down in their seats and stuck their legs in the air and ate their popcorn upside down. This is an age, of course, at which the esophagus can function without the aid of gravity.

A boy and girl on our right were having a spat. She tramped out on him, full of wrath, kicking me in the right ankle and dribbling root beer on my knees. She went back to him, though. Four times. She had better, too. I happen to know another young lady was seeing him in her absence.

Finally I retreated in disorder. I threaded my way out to the lobby through the supply lines and bought a Coke and an Abba Zaba and stood against the wall and ate and drank. An usher kept a suspicious eye on me.

I thought back to the Saturday afternoons of my generation, with old Doug Fairbanks up there on the screen, scaling walls and vanquishing blackguards and rescuing beautiful women.

I felt like a square.

Some of our sociologists have discovered that most adolescents these days are members of the leisure class. They are free of parental domination, it is observed, but they're not yet working or married.

Becoming a member of the leisure class is an ambition I have yet to realize, being only one-third qualified. I'm free of parental domination, but I'm married, and I work.

It is consoling, though, to have a couple of children who have made it. The parent always likes to see his issue attain his own lost goals.

There's a difference between mere idleness and true creative leisure. The man of leisure is always in pursuit of some end, though its nature may be subtle indeed.

I checked up on our own sons one summer morning to see how they were spending this golden time of youth.

Doug was spread-eagled on the patio, his face to the sun.

"Is this the way you plan to spend the summer?" I asked. "Loafing?"

"I'm not loafing, Pa," he said. "I'm tanning."

I found Curt in the dining room dismantling a machine on the table.

"What's that you're tearing apart," I asked. "My clock radio again?"

"It's my aquarium pump," he said.

"I thought you'd given up the care and feeding of tropical fish."

"An aquarium takes leisure time," he said. "It's my project for the summer."

The leisure class doesn't rise early. When my alarm buzzed the next morning, nobody else stirred. I got up and prepared for my day in unhurried quiet. Before leaving for work I tapped my wife on the shoulder.

"I'm going to work now," I said.

She opened one eye. "Awrumph," she said, quite clearly, and closed the eye.

I went into the living room. "Goodbye," I called out to the boys. "I'm going to work now."

There was an aristocratic groan from one of their rooms, then silence. One of the dogs, sleeping in my chair, raised an eyebrow, snorted, and sank back to sleep.

I drove to work faster than usual. Somebody has to support the leisure class.

I have discovered that the teen-ager's natural affinity for leisure reaches its zenith when he is first infused by that phenomenon known as the intellectual awakening.

Overnight they drop their playthings and pick up such bright baubles as Kierkegaard, Sartre, and Salinger. Naturally, we are eager for the innocents to stop counting their toes and get on with life's more difficult problems. But this long-awaited flowering is not an unqualified boon.

Once the muses have kissed the lad's brow it's hard to get him to do any manual labor around the house at all. The spark that ignites the higher brain centers seems to paralyze the back.

It is not easy to call him in from the dazzling woods in which he now walks with new gods. What father could summon his child from a romp on Olympus with Whitman, Hemingway, and Edna St. Vincent Millay to mow an earthly lawn?

Still, a household's wheels must turn, even if it means yanking heads down from the clouds, among which, like airplanes, they have been refueling at rarefied heights.

One of these emergencies arose one weekend. My wife brought it to our attention. That has been one of woman's functions since neolithic times—calling the male away from his abstract intellectualizing to fix something that leaked, clanked, clogged, or otherwise upset her sense of order.

She said the second level needed mowing. I put my book down. I had been reading *The City in History,* by Lewis Mumford, about how prehistoric woman seduced outdoor man away from the wilderness to a slothful life of gourmandizing and carnality in the first villages.

I went out and looked at the lawn. It had a beard like a goat. The boys were in their rooms. I rapped on one door. "How about mowing the lawn?" I called.

"Now?" came the answer. "I'm reading *Arrowsmith.*"

"*Arrowsmith!*" What a book that had been! It almost decided me on a career in biochemistry.

"What do you think of Dr. Gottlieb?" I shouted through the door.

"Great," he said. "I wish I had him for a teacher."

I knocked on the other door. I didn't want to tear a tender mind away from Max Gottlieb.

"How about mowing the lawn?" I called.

"Right now? I'm reading Jung."

"Not Jung," I said, "it's a Y sound. Like in Clara Kimball Young. What are you reading by him?"

"It's called *Jung on Life After Death,*" he said, "in the *Atlantic* magazine."

I decided to mow the lawn myself. It seemed brutal to call anyone back from a visit to Dr. Jung's hereafter.

The mower was out of gas. I went back to Mumford. He says our machines are choking us to death.

I'M A VETERINARIAN, NOT A PSYCHIATRIST

My wife's war with the dogcatcher was a fascinating study in tactics, fortitude, and conflicting ideologies.

It was her war. I was strictly an observer.

What made the struggle worth watching was the high degree of ability on both sides. The dogcatcher who worked our hill was a respectable antagonist—vigilant and efficient and not easily hoodwinked. But he had his match in my wife. He knew he was in a fight.

Once she was in the thing, she demonstrated an unexpected cunning and courage and a brash contempt for the strict letter of the law. Like most women, she simply sets aside minor commandments which she finds personally inconvenient.

So she suspended the leash law, but the dogcatcher didn't, and therein lay the contest.

The ground rules were complicated by there being not one but two dogs in the game, both large, shaggy, and remarkably stupid. One was our mongrel female sheepdog, an undisputed moron called Shag, and her psychopathic son, Blaze, a red brute with the build of a Labrador retriever and the brain of a crocodile.

My wife at one time did make a conscientious effort to keep these monsters under leash, but it was a crashing fiasco.

Shag got her chain intricately entangled in the power lawn mower and knocked over the barbecue, and Blaze very nearly strangled himself by winding his chain as tight as a bowstring around the clothes pole.

Besides, the two of them howled and carried on and fixed lugubrious eyes on all who passed by, giving my wife a strong sense of guilt. The leash experiment died ignobly.

The next phase of the struggle was pure anarchy. She just let the dogs have their thick heads.

That was when they discovered school. Great sport. Kids, games, snacks from lunch boxes.

But a heartless schoolteacher called the pound one day and the dogcatcher raced up the hill and made the pinch.

That hurt, but my wife's a good loser. She got in the car and went down to the pound and bailed the idiots out for four dollars and fifty cents each.

Then she tackled the thing head on. She organized an alarm system of housewives spotted strategically over the hill.

Soon it was a common experience to pick up the phone and hear the stirring cry, "The dogcatcher is coming!"

That was the signal to hop in the car and rush up the hill to the schoolhouse and wrangle the beasts before the dogcatcher got there.

This worked splendidly until one day some lady left her post; or perhaps the dogcatcher, sensing that he was being outwitted, chose some unexpected and devious route.

In any case the warning was not sounded in time and the two miscreants wound up in the pound again, looking sad and stupid.

The bill was only one-fifty this time, since their licenses were in order, but it was a humiliating setback. Yet the worst was ahead.

In time a summons came in the mail ordering my wife to appear in court to answer to the charge of violating the leash law.

This certainly was a cruel stroke. It was her first appearance before the bar of justice and she trembled with apprehension.

But she put on her best garments, locked the dogs in the house and went down to face it. She waited her turn among petty thieves and grifters and streetwalkers and pleaded guilty.

"What's this?" the judge asked when my wife's name was called and she walked forward. He looked her up and down, judicially. "Another—"

"No, no, your honor!" the city attorney interjected. "This is a leash law violation."

"I see," said the judge solemnly. "Well, how do you plead, Mrs.—uh—Smith?"

"Guilty, your honor," she squeaked.

"Well, Mrs. Smith," the judge said, "I'm sure you aren't a—ah—criminal, heh, heh, but these leash law violations are violations of the law, like anything else. I'm going to have to make an example of you, I'm afraid. Ten dollars or five days."

She got ten dollars out of her purse and paid the fine at the clerk's counter.

"Why didn't you do the five days and save your money?" I asked her when we were outside. "The boys and I could have got along all right."

We never knew how old Shag was. We had found her on the street eight or ten years back and brought her home because she was so shaggy. She stayed on. Shag always seemed an unimaginative name for a dog, especially one with no breeding. But she was so shaggy there was nothing else to call her. Any other name would have been a transparent denial of the obvious.

She had a limp, probably the result of a brush with a car. Part of her upper lip had been chewed away, so that a couple of fangs were constantly bared. Strangers were never sure whether she was angry or amused.

She only had one trick. She could sit and stare you in the eye until your nerves cracked, the way children turn around and stare you down in church. If your face betrayed a trace of compassion she limped over and put her wet muzzle, with the two naked fangs, in your hand.

She was such an unprepossessing creature that we were dumfounded that first year when she whelped. It was a testament to the incredible power of nature. I have always suspected that the father was drunk. In any case he was certainly a ne'er-do-well. We never saw him after the *fait accompli*.

There were eight in the litter. Giving them away was one of the most difficult tasks I have ever undertaken. I passed off most of them in a neighborhood saloon frequented by threadbare folk of clouded judgment but warm heart. I had to buy a lot of drinks.

Outside of motherhood, Shag had only one other claim to nobility in this life. Some of the neighborhood kids said she was just about as good a second base as there was in baseball. She didn't *play* second base, you understand. She actually *was* second base.

We kept one of the pups, an impulsive decision I was later to regret a thousand times. We called him Blaze, because he had a white blaze on his forehead. He was a red Labrador retriever, a remarkable achievement for the son of a blue mongrel sheepdog and a stray half-breed chow.

We always excused ourselves for keeping him with the theory that he might turn into a good watchdog. He was, in fact, as dangerous as a welcome mat. He pretended to guard the front porch. When a stranger walked up he would roll over on his back and wave his paws in the air. He barked only at the moon and shooting stars and foreign cars.

If any trouble came up, Blaze ran and got his mother, who was more aggressive. She was fond of Blaze, but overprotective. She barked at his female friends.

But I always tried to do my best for the miserable curs. A man must take care of his own creatures. Nobody else is going to shoe his children or wash his dogs.

I actually helped wash the dogs one Sunday afternoon. Fleas were gaining the upper hand. The dogs had become finical at table. One ignored his persimmon cake.

I got some dog soap and told the boys to fill the bucket with warm water.

"Pa," said Doug, "you better catch the dogs before they see us with the bucket."

I told them not to worry. I've always been influential with dogs. I'm not afraid of them. They know that and are not afraid of me.

They respect me and will do anything for me that isn't against their nature. I wouldn't, for example, ask a dog to remain chaste or come home early on Saturday night.

I went out to the patio and whistled. The dogs bounded out of the bush and skidded up to my feet. They commenced scratching. The boys came out the door with the bucket and brush.

Shag started to skulk away, affecting nonchalance. I lunged for her. She spurted out of my clutches and ran for it.

Old Shag ran with her head low and canted to the right. Her right ear rode close to the ground. It was some kind of rheumatism. She was the only dog I know who listened to tracks instead of scenting them.

"Never mind her," I told the boys. "Let's get Blaze."

Blaze was bigger than Shag and just as shaggy. Like an owl, he was ninety percent feathers. He was, to say the least, emotionally immature. He was supposed to be a Labrador retriever but never showed the least interest in retrieving anything, or work of any kind, for that matter. He was a sex psychopath.

We held him by his collar and legs. We poured water over him and lathered him. He shrank to half his size. He threw back his head and launched a lachrymose solo.

I believe the poor brute was attempting the aria *Vesti la giubba* from *Pagliacci,* although he was not a natural tenor.

Across the canyon old Shag set up a sympathetic obbligato in what she apparently fancied was a soprano. It was hideous. I sent Curt after her.

Blaze was a mass of iridescent foam. He quit singing and began snapping at the bubbles that floated up from his nose. I rinsed him off and dried him with a beach towel.

"He's shivering," Doug said. "I'll get him something to wear." He took the dog in the house.

Curt staggered up with Shag struggling in his arms. We subdued her and were scrubbing her when Blaze sauntered out of the house. He looked freshened and debonair. He was wearing a striped shirt and red Bermuda shorts. Every inch a *boulevardier*.

"Look, Pa," said Doug. "Maurice Chevalier."

I stood up to admire Blaze and relaxed my grip on Shag. She wrenched free, shook herself mightily and streaked off over the hill toward the Daltons and asylum. Blaze bounded after her with a yelp of virile joy.

We sat down on the steps in despair. In a while the phone rang. It was Dalton.

"Say," he said, "I think your dogs went by here a minute ago. Was one of them wearing Bermuda shorts?"

"Yes, yes," I said impatiently. "Which way'd they go?"

"Don't know," said Dalton. "But I'll tell you one thing. You better go after 'em. The one the other one was chasing didn't have a stitch on."

I tried to get rid of Blaze through the Society for Prevention of Cruelty to Animals. It was one of my darker chapters.

He was driving me out of my mind. It's the only explanation I can offer. We had taken him to the dog and cat hospital half a dozen times, asking if something couldn't be done about his psychosomatic ailments.

Finally the veterinarian threw up his hands. "I'm a veterinarian, Mr. Smith," he sighed, "not a psychiatrist. I can't take your money any more."

I certainly couldn't afford to have the brute psychoanalyzed. That's something I've even had to deny myself. I decided to take him under personal psychiatric observation.

Anyone who has taken high school psychology could have diagnosed his trouble quickly enough. The dog had a cyclothymic personality bordering on a manic depressive psychosis, with an anxiety neurosis and a mild megalomania.

The main symptoms were his failure to accept housebreaking, an obsessive wanderlust, and the delusion that all his problems could be barked away. We had to tie him to the pepper tree, which he immediately dug up.

So in desperation I took him to the SPCA and asked them to find him a good home with a fenced yard.

"One of us has to leave my hearth," I explained. I left him there and drove bravely home.

"What have you done with the dog?" my wife asked. She can sense sin. I confessed.

"It's for the best," I explained. "He'll find somebody with a fenced yard. Somebody who understands emotional illness."

I won't describe the rest of that weekend. It was ghastly.

On Wednesday the SPCA called.

"You better come after your dog, Mr. Smith," the man said. "Or we'll have to . . ."

"No! No!" I cried. "Not that! I'm in trouble enough already!"

"Well," he said, "I see you signed a 'No PTS' card. But we can't hold him much longer. We just haven't got the room."

My flesh turned cold. PTS is a euphemism, of course, for Put to Sleep, which is a euphemism for—I couldn't let myself think of it.

"My God!" I cried. "You don't know what you're saying! Listen to me. If that dog is—PTS'd—my life is ruined. You hear? I'll have to shoot myself."

"We'll hold him till Sunday," the man said.

I went after the dog on Sunday. The board bill was eight dollars. That put us right back where we started, plus costing me eight dollars, a week of emotional stress and some of the love and esteem in which I was once held.

My wife said there were dark corners in my heart she never knew were there before.

EVERYBODY CAN'T BE A MAZEROSKI

A loud thump against the side of the house awoke me from a spring nap. There was a rustling in the ivy outside my window and an eerie patter, as of elves playing in a wood.

I yanked back the curtain and peered red-eyed into the hostile day.

"What is it!" I shouted. "What's going on?"

A small girl arose from the acanthus plant. She was the height of a lamp table, with a tomato face and buckskin hair.

"Who are you?" she said. "Mrs. Smith's father?"

"Never mind that!" I barked. "Who're *you?*"

She held up a muddy ball. "I'm the catcher," she said.

So that was it. Baseball was back. The asphalt league. There was no use trying to sleep. Home plate is at the edge of the street above the bedroom window. I got up and went out to watch the game.

I first got mixed up in baseball the year the Pittsburgh Pirates won the pennant. Before that fantastic season I hadn't the slightest idea what an RBI or an ERA was, or a sacrifice, or why an infield fly is sometimes an automatic out.

My personal involvement arose from the discovery that the game was being played in our street with a tennis ball. As naïve as I was, I still knew this was wrong. I drove down to the Thrifty Drug Store and bought the neighborhood a real baseball.

Having thus made myself a hero, I was invited to watch a game. There was nothing in my experience, and surely nothing in the rule book, to account for what I saw that day.

My son Douglas, who was then perhaps the world's greatest centerfielder with baby teeth, was pitching to a neighbor boy I had never seen before, but who must have weighed 160 pounds.

The catcher was a pine tree. It turned out to be erratic.

Doug blazed a fast one over and the big neighbor boy proved as unco-ordinated as he was heavy. He missed the pitch and so did the pine tree.

After a raucous argument over the protocol of the situation, the pitcher had to fetch the ball himself, making a hazardous descent into the canyon and its forest of poison oak. There is, I believe, nothing in the rule book to sanction this.

I had no idea where first base was until a frail lad with long red hair and thick eyeglasses got a good piece of the Thrifty Drug Store ball on a soft pitch and ran for first. First base turned out to be Victoria, the little girl next door. She was wearing a mitt the size of a sofa cushion.

Victoria was so unnerved by the actual occurrence of anything as improbable as a base hit that she flung herself wildly into the air, skirts and blond pigtails flying, and missed the ball entirely. An error is an error, and nobody would have said an unkind word to Victoria, I'm sure. But she sat down on the curb and began to cry.

Meanwhile, the red-haired lad who had got the base hit had dropped his eyeglasses and couldn't find second base, which was our dog Shag. At this point the pitcher walked manfully over to first base and sat down on the curb beside the weeping Victoria.

"Vickie girl," he said, looking wretchedly into his glove, "don't cry. Everybody can't be a Mazeroski."

"I just *hate* baseball!" she sobbed.

By this time the lad who had got the base hit had stumbled onto second base and pounded on to third, which was wide open at the moment because the third baseman, unknown to everybody else, had been called home by his mother.

There was a strident debate over whether the runner was entitled to take a base while the pitcher was comforting the first baseman. He was made to go back to second and the pitcher was given a balk.

All hands stood idle while a Jaguar, a Plymouth, and a Ford pickup went by, and then they got back to the old ball game. Next up was a raven-haired girl who had eyes the size of a baseball but couldn't hit one with a breadboard. I sensed that Doug was pitching easy to her, and accused him of it. He lost his poise.

"What would you do, Pa," he demanded, "if you had a pine tree for a catcher?"

Mazeroski, I learned soon enough, was the name of a young man who played second base that vintage year for the Pirates, and who was, consequently, one of that season's demigods.

Our son's passion for the Pirates was an embarrassment at first. Our block was full of Dodger people, and the boy's defection was hard to explain.

What went wrong? Where did we fail? I couldn't afford to consult a psychiatrist, but I know one socially. I mentioned the problem casually one evening at a cocktail party.

"Obviously, Smith," he said, "the child has a Pirate-directed simplex," or words to that effect. "He needs guidance. Try to get him interested in the Cincinnati Reds. All they need is some pitching."

When the Reds came to town to play the Dodgers I took Doug to the game. He was, at least, polite. After each home run, by either side, he clapped his hands in the perfunctory manner of a plumber applauding a *pas de deux* at the ballet. His *emotions* were not involved.

In the beginning I mistook his *malaise* for a premature intellectual awakening. We often saw him sitting in his room in silence, apparently tuned in on some far-out world. This, I thought, was a sign. He was swimming out in the universe of ideas. His swift young mind for the first time was chasing the elusive nymph of pure thought in the bright woods of reason.

One evening when I surprised him in such a reverie, however, I discovered that his right ear was only six inches from his transistor radio, which was turned down so low it couldn't be heard at any distance. He was listening to the Pirates and the Giants.

It was later in that remarkable season that Douglas discovered his occult power. It has always grieved me that I didn't have faith in him when he told me the Pirates were going to win the flag. Nobody else gave the team a chance.

"They'll win, Pa," he assured me.

I tried to disabuse him. A parent wants to shield a tender child from disappointment. One hates to see their beliefs shattered.

"Doug," I told him, "be realistic. It just isn't in the cards."

He merely shook his head. He felt sorry for me.

How could a small boy foresee the outcome of the National League race that year against all the sound thinking in the country, including mine?

It was, I learned later, a combination of voodoo, extrasensory perception, remote control, and blind faith.

One night when the Pirates were playing the Cardinals, and were down two to one in the eighth inning, I caught him working his black art. He was sitting in the big chair in his room, rigid as a statue. His head was tilted to one side. He was staring at the ceiling. The light was off. I thought he was in a trance, or perhaps having a reaction to his tetanus shot.

"What goes on here!" I cried in alarm.

"I'm trying to get Danny Murtaugh to put in Elroy Face," he said.

I knew by that time that Murtaugh was the field manager of the Pirates and Elroy their star relief pitcher. He explained that whenever Pittsburgh was in hot water he always sat in exactly that position, and then Murtaugh would send Elroy in and the day was saved.

He said he had to get the word through by mental telepathy because it would be too expensive to telephone Pittsburgh, and he doubted if Danny Murtaugh would accept a collect call.

"He doesn't know who I am yet," he explained.

I was disturbed. I don't like to see the dark clouds of superstition rising in a child's psyche.

"I guess it's all right to love a baseball team," I told him, "but don't let superstition get a hold on you."

"It's not superstition, Pa," he said. "I don't believe in that stuff. It's just that when I sit this way the Pirates usually win."

"What about the times you sit that way and they don't win?"

"Pa," he said, "you can't win 'em all."

Baseball does give a father and son something they can talk about on common ground. That incredible season I used to get the paper off the front porch in the mornings and wake him up to discuss the scores.

I regard the early morning hours as the best time for conversation. The mind is refreshed and alert. However, not everybody's chemistry is like mine.

One morning, I remember, I turned back to the sports page and found that the Pirates had come from behind again to win in the ninth inning. That was their specialty.

I went into Doug's room and rattled the sports pages in his face. "Wake up!" I said. "The Pirates got beat again last night."

"Pa," he said, "don't kid me. Dick Stuart hit a home run in the ninth and they won."

That was when I discovered that he was sleeping with his radio. I believe he absorbed the baseball scores in his sleep. Electronics has spoiled this generation.

"Why can't you read under the covers with a flashlight like I used to?" I asked him. "Develop your mind."

"I do," he said. "See?" He slipped a book out from under his pillow. It was *The Baseball Annual for 1960*.

"Don't you ever think of anything besides baseball?" I said.

"You'll be glad someday," he said, "when I'm a bonus baby."

"Bonus baby? What's that?"

"That's when a major league team finds a good high school player and gives him one hundred thousand dollars just to sign him up. I'm going to give you and Ma my bonus. I can live off my salary."

"That's pretty darn generous of you," I said. I let him go back to sleep. If he was going to be a bonus baby he needed it.

It wasn't until the second day of the World Series (in which, it is now recorded for posterity, the Pittsburgh Pirates defeated the New York Yankees) that I found out he was taking his transistor radio to school to listen to the games.

He set out that morning with what appeared to be only his books, his lunch, a yellow zinnia for the teacher and his monthly new pair of tennis shoes, which were already exhausted and black.

He was humming. Something made me suspicious. It was all too casual. Under sharp interrogation he confessed he had the radio in his sack lunch.

"How come?" I demanded.

He explained that the transistor radio was operated by batteries and kept his tuna sandwich warm.

I certainly didn't fall for that transparent deceit. Anybody knows a tuna sandwich is better cold.

"You can't take your radio to school," I said.

"Why not? Last year the teacher had one in her drawer."

"That was a Dodger year," I explained.

"I thought this was a democracy," he said.

He left home without his radio. And yet, at dinnertime he seemed oddly well-informed on the details and heroics of the day's game.

"If it was you, Pa," he said, "would you try to make third from first on a line-drive single to right field?"

Well naturally I wouldn't. I would have stopped at second. But that wasn't the real issue.

"You seem to know a lot of details about today's game for a boy who was supposed to be in school," I observed. "How does that happen?"

"The teacher told us what happened after every inning," he said. "She had a radio in her drawer. Nobody told *her* she couldn't bring it to school."

So when the ball hit the house and I looked out the window and saw the little girl in the acanthus bush I had to go outdoors and see what kind of a spring we were going to have.

It was mostly the same old gang, but a couple of seasons older. And there were some new faces up from the minors. Victoria was at bat. Young Harvey Gribble was on the mound. Our dog Blaze and a small girl were catching. She was the girl I saw through the window. Her name turned out to be Susu Katz.

The Gribble boy wound up and pitched. Victoria swung and missed. Even so, I could see that Victoria was not the same ballplayer she had been a season or two ago. She had developed something I'd never noticed before. Aplomb, perhaps.

Then the Gribble boy gave her a slow ball. She belted it into the new steel link fence of the Self Realization Fellowship across the street. Doug scooped it up on a bounce and threw to Athena at the fire plug, which had been designated first base for the season.

Athena caught the toss nicely and Victoria was out. I remembered how Athena had looked out there once. All pigtails, elbows, and kneecaps. She couldn't catch with a knitting bag. And now, I could see, she had become a very mature first baseman indeed.

A girl on a tricycle kept wheeling around the infield. A ragdoll redhead type and her grubby brother were playing tug-of-war with an innertube. When the fielding team came in to bat I spoke to Doug about the little ones.

"You ought to keep them out of the way," I said. "They'll get hurt."

"They won't listen, Pa," he said. "They're a menace."

"Where do they come from, anyway?"

"I don't know. They're a new batch. There's more every year. I may quit baseball. It's getting too crowded."

Susu went into her windup. The pitch was high and outside, but the Gribble boy got a piece of it and drilled one out to the fence. He ran for the fire hydrant. The little girl on the tricycle and the redhead and her grubby brother began jumping up and down and shouting.

"Rah rah *rhee!* Kick'm in the *knee!* Rah rah *razz!* Kick'm in the *other* knee!"

Then they all fell down in the street and gave themselves up to paroxysms of giggling.

"Good Lord!" I whispered to Doug. "Where'd they learn that?"

"*I* taught it to them, Pa," he said. "I thought maybe it would keep them quiet. I learned it at leadership camp."

When the score was twenty-two to nine I went back inside and lay down. I dozed off. I dreamed that our son Douglas, grown to manhood, came home in a red Thunderbird and presented his mother and me with a check for one hundred thousand dollars from the Pittsburgh Pirates, while a chorus of redheads sang "Rah rah *rhee,* kick'm in the *knee!*"

And every once in a while there was a loud thump against the house.

DON'T WORRY, THE TRAIN WILL WAIT

Getting my wife off to the PTA convention in San Francisco was enervating work. The tempo of activity began to speed up a week before her departure.

She stayed up every night until two or three o'clock, sewing on her wardrobe. Her sewing always keeps me awake. If she worked on the sewing machine constantly, I could get used to it. A soldier learns to sleep on a battlefield. But now and then she stops sewing to use the pinking shears. It's the pinking shears that wake me up.

"What about the laundry?" I asked her. "Are you going to do it Monday before you leave?" I have a horror of being without clean underwear.

"No. I'm going to do it Sunday so I can iron Monday."

"What about our meals?"

"I'm making out a list. There's a dozen pounds of hamburger in the freezer. There are three TV dinners for one night and a whole lot of frozen Mexican food for another."

"It's been my experience," I said, "that Mexican food doesn't freeze very well. Especially enchiladas."

She ignored me. "How cold is it in San Francisco?" she asked. "I don't know what coat to take."

"How do I know how cold it is in San Francisco?" I said. "Besides, it isn't always the same. Some days it's colder than others."

I got the weather section of the paper and looked up San Francisco in the temperature tables.

"The minimum in San Francisco yesterday," I informed her, "was 59."

"Oh," she said. "How cold is that?"

"Well, boiling is 212 degrees and freezing is 32. Figure it out for yourself."

She went outdoors and began pulling at the weeds.

"Why are you doing that?" I asked. "I thought you were too cramped for time."

"I have to get four days ahead with the weeds," she explained, "or when I get back I'll never catch up."

Among all my other chores, I had to get up early the day of her departure and drive her to the Glendale railroad station.

She put on her hat and gloves and gave one last look around. The boys were already off to school. I was already late to work.

"Do you think you can manage?" she said.

"Don't worry about us," I said. "We'll make out like the Swiss Family Robinson."

"The Robinsons had a woman in the house," she said. Women hate to think any male, however healthy and ingenious, can survive twenty-four hours without them, even in benevolent weather.

"They had a woman," I said, "but they didn't have a blender, a disposer, a milkman, a dry-cleaning man, an automatic dishwasher, a dozen pounds of frozen hamburger, a telephone, a clock radio, two bicycles, an automobile, two dogs and a cat."

"And frozen enchiladas," she added.

She sneaked one last look in the mirror and stooped to pick some lint off the rug.

"As I remember," she said, "they had a cat."

"That may be," I granted. "You'll miss your train."

She started reciting the Don't Forgets.

"Don't forget," she said, "to set the alarm and wake the boys and put the water on and unlock the back door for the milkman."

"Don't worry," I said. "You'll miss your train."

"Don't forget," she said, "to turn off the stove and the heater, if it's on, and lock the doors and put the dogs out, poor things."

"Don't worry," I said. "You'll miss your train."

"Don't worry," she said. "The train will wait."

I believe she thought it actually would wait. The PTA is a powerful organization.

She looked in the mirror and adjusted her hat. She started in on the Where Things Ares.

"There are some clean bath towels in the closet. I left some chicken pies in the freezer. The detergent is under the sink."

"Don't worry," I said. "I'll make out like Robinson Crusoe."

We got the bags in the car and headed for the station. She kept looking back at the house. It didn't catch fire. She seemed surprised.

"You can have the leftover meat loaf tonight," she said. "Just heat it up. Set the oven at 350 degrees."

She fell silent, poking through her purse for a lipstick.

"Is that all the How to Dos?" I asked.

"The whats?"

"The How to Dos. How to Do this, How to Do that."

"Oh," she said. "Boiled eggs. You put the eggs in a kettle of cold water and when it comes to a boil the eggs are three-minute."

"Science is wonderful," I said.

"And don't forget," she said, "if you have any trouble, phone me."

"We better send a postcard," I said. "I'm not sure if we know how to use the telephone. Do you plug it in and turn a crank or something?"

"All right, I'm sorry," she said. "But you never do any little things around the house. How do I know if you know how?"

"Don't worry," I said. "Have a good time."

She caught the train. I think it waited for her a little. She got away before I could ask her what detergent is for.

It is a cliché of literature, as well as of the movies, TV, and real life that when the cook walks out disaster walks in.

Ordinarily self-reliant people panic and run around the house with their hands in the air crying, "The cook has quit—what will become of us?"

This scene always annoys me. Surely man's first instinct was to forage and prepare a meal fit for human consumption. It should be as easy for modern man as trimming a hedge or adjusting a carburetor.

If the preparation of food was not a built-in human skill, our species would have been stamped out by the dinosaurs and man would never have survived to paint lovely, graceful animals on the walls of dark caves and make hydrogen bombs.

After my wife left for the convention we were expected to panic and run up and down the neighborhood crying, "The cook has quit—what will become of us?"

We are made of harder metal. I merely waited until she was well out of town and then phoned a woman I happen to know who will come in and cook and clean up on a minute's notice.

She said she was sorry, but she had already got a minute's notice from another man. "It's an emergency, Mr. Smith," she explained. "His wife is gone to some PTA convention." As the poet Homer said (*circa* 800 B.C.) "No trust is to be placed in women."

I turned my back on the entire sex and stopped on the way home at a supermarket. I know how to survive. I picked up two boxes of frozen meatballs and two cans of spaghetti and lined up at the checkout counter.

"Well, Mr. Smith," said the checkout girl. She knows me from cashing checks for me the day before payday. "We're certainly going to have meatballs tonight, aren't we?"

"Do you think I have bought too many meatballs?" I asked. I'm never too proud to seek the advice of experts.

"Well," she said, "there's twenty meatballs in each box. That's forty meatballs. It's up to you, Mr. Smith. If you can eat forty meatballs you're in business."

"Wrap them up," I said.

The boys were delighted. They agreed that meatballs were an imaginative choice. I suggested we cook only twenty. They argued that it would be wise to cook the whole mess, because if any were left over, which they said was unlikely, they could be kept for lunch, dogs, snacks, and guests.

We cooked the forty. You have to keep tumbling them in the pan so they won't stick and burn. When they are brown all over you slop in the two cans of spaghetti with meat sauce.

This is the critical moment. If the pan isn't too small, so the spaghetti spills over, or too hot, so the meatballs stick, and burn, and the telephone doesn't ring, then you are in business.

As it turned out, the pan was somewhat small and too hot and the telephone rang.

So there was something for the dogs after all, which was a good thing because I had forgot dog food when I was out foraging.

We accounted for the entire forty meatballs. Everyone agreed it was a tribute to my foresight and judgment.

We finally got a woman in to help out, after all. It wasn't really my idea.

My older son telephoned me at the office one desperate afternoon.

"Pa," he whispered hoarsely, "Margo is here."

"Margo?" I said. "Margo who?" I couldn't remember any Margo, outside the movies.

"She's the girl you don't know," he said. "She's in my class. She's the one I told you got an A in social science."

"Oh, of course," I said. "*That* Margo. Is she in trouble? What does she want?"

"She wants to wash the dishes," he said.

"For Pete's sake!" I exclaimed. "You know better than to phone me when I'm busy over such an inconsequential matter as that. Does she know where the soap is?"

"She's already started washing them," he said. "What shall I do? I told her you might not want her to wash our dishes. I told her you're very independent."

"Listen," I said, "what will be will be. As the Italians say, *que sera sera*. Right? I wouldn't want to *ask* her to do the dishes, but if she's already started I wouldn't want to ask her to *stop*. Women are very sensitive that way. You have to make them feel useful. They have a deep-seated sense of inadequacy."

"Okay, Pa," he said. "I'll tell her that."

"No, no!" I shouted. "Don't tell her *that!* It would only *add* to her sense of inadequacy. You see?"

"I think so," he said.

"She wants to wash the dishes," I explained, "because it gives her a *raison d'être*. We can't take that away from her, can we, sport?"

"I guess not," he said.

"So let her wash the dishes," I counseled. "Let her express herself as a woman. And listen, tell her don't forget the pots and pans. You hear?"

"Okay," he said. "Can I go to the ball game on my bicycle?"

"Not while Margo is washing the dishes," I told him. "Women won't wash dishes if there is no man there to watch them. They want you to feel guilty. If you go to the ball game on your bicycle, she'll probably quit washing dishes and go out and buy a hat or something. We can't afford that kind of a complication."

"Okay," he said. "What's for dinner?"

"Abalone," I said. "The fruit of the sea. The succulent gastropod taken from the shoreline where the struggle for existence is most fierce and primitive."

"Gee, Pa," he said, "did you catch it yourself?"

"It comes in a can," I explained.

"Oh. Can I go to the ball game on my bicycle after dinner?"

"Yes," I said. "If your homework is done and the lawn is mowed. And the dishes are done."

"Don't worry about the dishes," he said.

I went home with a singing heart. The dishes were done, and a good job, too. But she had forgotten the pots and pans. Women are all the same.

My wife came home from the convention on Saturday. She took a cab from the station. The boys spent the morning cleaning house. It was an astonishing performance. When they finished they invited me to make a tour of inspection. Everything was remarkably shipshape.

They had vacuumed the carpet and rearranged the furniture with geometric precision. The records were put away. The paper was folded on the cocktail table. The furniture was dusted. The chic throw pillows were set symmetrically on the sofa.

"Incredible!" I exclaimed.

In the kitchen everything had been scrubbed spotless. The sink tile gleamed. Even the range was clean. No drop of grease or crumb of bread marred its surface. No dish or glass or knife or spoon was in sight. The dish towel hung as nobly as Caesar's toga from its rack.

"Incredible!" I said again. "Great work, boys. You might as well go out and play now, and I'll just wait for your mother."

When they were gone I looked around again. It would never do. There are insights involved in living with a woman that are beyond childish perception. Children don't know that beating a housewife at her own game is a grievous sin.

I went into the kitchen and looked in the cupboard. Peanut butter struck me as ideal for the task at hand. I made a toasted peanut butter sandwich. I burned the toast and scraped it on the tile work table. I used too much peanut butter, so that when I squeezed the top slice of toast down, some of it oozed out on the tile.

I got a glass of milk and left the bottle on the sink. I went in the living room and lay down on the couch and went through the paper, eating my peanut butter sandwich. As I tired of each section of the paper, I gave it a fling. No two sections fell in the same place.

I had just put my sandwich crusts on the cocktail table when she walked in with the boys.

"Well, *gee!*" she said in a burst of homecoming good will. "Everything looks so clean and *tidy!*"

The boys took in my handiwork. They looked puzzled and betrayed. I winked. "Wait," I whispered.

"We wanted it spotless," I told my wife, "but it's impossible to keep up with everything."

"Don't I know it!" she bubbled. She picked up my peanut butter crusts and hustled them off to the kitchen, humming.

"Why this looks marvelous!" she sang out from the kitchen. "It won't take me two minutes to get everything in order."

The boys looked at me in unabashed filial admiration.

DON'T GIVE UP, WHATE'ER YOU DO

A spring day of a certain quality moves the human race, especially women, to clean house and change everything about. It must be a dry, windy, and limpid day.

We had such a day. Most everything we had collected through the winter with acquisitive zeal was disposed of. The trouble is that nothing was really lost or destroyed. It merely changed ownership.

No matter how worn and trifling a thing may be, it will find a friend in our house before it is consigned to the trash box.

With deep reluctance I parted with an old cowboy hat. It never fit me, and Curt had grown up to it. In exchange for the hat I acquired two complete years of the *National Geographic* magazine, somewhat dog-eared.

I also gave up a self-portrait painted in oil one evening three years previously when my wife was at a PTA meeting. For my portrait I took a nine-gallon aquarium that no longer holds water.

Some exciting trades were made between the boys. A set of ball bearings of mixed sizes was exchanged evenly for a 1958 World Almanac and a used typewriter ribbon.

I wanted the ball bearings myself, but couldn't make a deal. I was especially embittered by the recollection that I had traded the 1958 World Almanac at our last spring housecleaning and got nothing for it but a triple-color ball-point pen. It has since run out of ink in all three colors.

The typewriter ribbon also once was my possession, but I threw it in the junk box, from which it obviously was retrieved and used against me.

My wife is a shrewd spring trader but unfortunately she never has much to bargain with but peculiarly female things such as ranunculus bulbs, old petit point pieces, and recipes cut from *McCall's*.

Even so, she didn't do badly this year. She convinced me that I could grow ranunculuses in the aquarium that won't hold water and traded me her bulbs for my tennis shoes, which she says she needs to garden in.

My sweetest coup was engineered from a position of strength. I had the derringer, a fine wall piece for any man's room. Curt got it, but only at the sacrifice of a striped blue and maroon necktie which I bought in Italy and hadn't seen since he borrowed it for the junior high school prom.

I nearly got my old tuxedo out of the house and into the junk box, but they caught me. They said I couldn't throw it away, it was too splendid and too full of memories.

"After all," my wife said, "we were married in it."

"*I* was married in it," I corrected. "You were in white."

She said she would be willing to trade me her gown for my tuxedo. I agreed, rather than have tears on a nice spring day. It worked out quite well. I left the tuxedo in the closet and she left the white gown in the cedar chest. Only the ownership had changed hands.

I tried to get rid of my old World War II uniform, too, but they wouldn't let me.

It was in the very back of the closet. It looked old and inglorious, with its vain little campaign bar across the chest.

"Why haven't we got rid of that thing long ago?" I asked my wife. "Given it to the Goodwill or something?"

"What would the Goodwill want with an old uniform?"

She had a point there. You can't easily give a uniform away. You have to burn it, like The Flag. I couldn't bring myself to do that.

I shut myself in the bedroom and tried it on. It may be in the grip of similar sentiments that women try on their old wedding gowns. Not with the idea of marrying again, but just to reassert a faded truth.

I was astounded. It fit nicely, except for a tightness in the shoulders. Apparently I've been putting on a little muscle in that region.

"Charming," my wife said. "You look like Field Marshal Montgomery."

I studied myself in the mirror. By Jove, there was something in what she said. Yes, it was the crow's feet and shafts of gray above the ears and a look of command, I thought, about the whole face.

"If they want me back," I said, "I shall demand a full colonelcy."

That's my military position at the moment, if anybody wants to know. And I have my own uniform.

For me, the hardest task of all is throwing out old books. But the time comes. I decided to do some weeding in my library, if a few hundred books scattered about as if washed up in a flood can be called a library.

My wife did the actual throwing away, but I made the decisions. She was dusting the books anyway, so I just asked her to read out the titles of any whose continuing worth she questioned.

"Get a cardboard box," I suggested, "and any books I don't want any more you can throw in. We'll give them to the Goodwill."

"All right," she said in a while, "what about this one? *A General Introduction to Psychoanalysis* by Sigmund Freud."

"We better keep it," I said. "Someday they'll get around to showing the movie on TV and you'll probably want to read the book."

She threw Freud in the box, a little harder than necessary, it seemed to me.

"What about *Just Folks,*" she said, "by Edgar Guest?"

"*Just Folks!* Where did that come from?"

"The Daltons gave it to you for your birthday. Remember? Or was it Ilya Ransome?"

I took *Just Folks* and thumbed through it.

"Listen to this," I said, reading a stanza from *See It Through.*

> *Black may be the clouds about you*
> *And your future may seem grim,*
> *But don't let your nerve desert you;*
> *Keep yourself in fighting trim.*

I tossed *Just Folks* in the box.

"What about this?" she said. *"They Pay Me to Catch Footballs* by Tommy McDonald of the Philadelphia Eagles?"

"In the box," I said. "I never cared for McDonald's style. Reminds me of Little Orphan Annie."

"I guess this one is past its usefulness," she said. *"How to Build and Operate a Model Railroad."*

Yes, our railroading era ended a few years ago, but it gave me a twinge when the book fell in the box.

She began to giggle. "How about this? *Facts of Life and Love for Teen-Agers?"*

"Where did that come from?" I asked.

"You bought it. Remember? You said there were things even you didn't know yet."

"Better hang onto it," I said. "I haven't finished it."

We threw away *How to Increase Sales and Put Yourself Across by Telephone* and *The New Speed-O-Gram Technique for Persuasive Public Speaking.*

But we held onto *How to Watch Birds* by Roger Barton, *The Plain Man's Guide to Wine,* and *In a New World* by Horatio Alger, Jr.

After we finished I looked through the box to see what we had managed to get rid of. Not much to show for an afternoon's work. I retrieved *Just Folks* from the pile and turned to the last stanza of *See It Through.*

> *You may fail, but fall still fighting;*
> *Don't give up, whate'er you do;*
> *Eyes front, head high to the finish.*
> *See it through!*

I put Edgar back on the shelf. You can't find inspiration like that in Sigmund Freud.

While the fever was on us we changed rooms about, too. My wife and I took the boys' room. Curt took our bedroom and Doug took the den.

"Every man needs a retreat," I explained to all hands. "A cave into which he can crawl when bested, lick his torn paws, curse his foes and escape womankind."

"I suppose so," she said.

"Boys should have a room of their own," I continued, "to learn the art of being alone, of surviving in an empty world on the broth of their own minds."

They were spellbound.

A room of his own! I reflected. A secret chamber in which his inner-most fancies may be loosed to try their wings and fling wild shadows against the walls. A temple of solitude in which he may learn self-discipline, order, mastery of his environment.

Inspired, we all pitched in to create these sanctums.

The operation was more difficult than we had foreseen. It posed fantastic problems in logistics.

The den is separated from the bedrooms by the living room and the bedrooms are separated from each other by a short hall.

The problem was to move all *our* furniture from our room into the boys' room, half the furniture from the boys' room into our room, and the other half into the den. Without banging into anything, of course. The den furniture meanwhile had to be moved into the living room.

The trouble, we found out, is that you can't move one bed to the place of another without first moving the other bed to the place of the first. This is absurd unless you can find someplace to put the second bed, temporarily, while the first bed is being moved into its place.

The key is the living room. It must be used to park articles en route from one place to another, while their successors are being moved to their old places. Yet at the same time the living room must be kept clear for passage of articles in transit.

Meanwhile, the living room has its own furniture, except for such articles as may be moved temporarily into one of the bedrooms, the den or the corridor, which must be kept clear at all times.

You can see it must be carefully thought out.

The feasibility of our entire program depended on the supposition that both my desk, from the den, and my wife's sewing table, from our old bedroom, would fit into the new bedroom. We tried the desk first. It is big, old, and heavy, of solid oak.

It would not go through the bedroom door. We removed the door. Once in the bedroom we set the desk down and rehung the door. We now saw clearly that the desk could not be put in its proposed place without removing a bulky chest of drawers. But this could not be moved out of the room without removing the desk, which now was in its way.

This required removing the door again. We removed the door. We put the desk back in the den. We then removed the chest of drawers. We found that this piece, however, could not be gotten into the den without first removing the desk.

This was our low-water mark.

But we tackled it. We moved the desk to the kitchen, which, of course, required removal of the kitchen door. We moved the chest of drawers into the den. We moved the desk into the bedroom. This was our first taste of victory, a satisfying moment indeed.

When we finished there were some charming oddities.

Doug, who now had the den, was probably one of the few red-blooded juveniles in America with a Picasso still life and a set of Havelock Ellis in his room.

In my new den, which was the bedroom, I had a complete set of *Boy's Life* for the previous four years and a picture of Old Glory in full color.

Curt was doing his homework at my wife's vanity. The television was sitting on her hope chest in the living room.

The sewing table was in the garage.

After Doug moved into the den we soon realized he would need a closet. When the house was built the den had none. The den then was actually a single attached garage. A single attached garage is as useful as an appendix. We weren't in the house six months before the garage began to look like a war surplus store. One couldn't open the door without it banging into a pre-World War II sofa my wife was going to upholster someday.

So we had to build a double garage and convert the single attached garage into a den. Today we can't even get a single car in the double garage because of the sofa, which remains un-upholstered, and many other priceless relics of the ante-bellum period.

We had to put a closet in the den after Doug finally got the knack of hanging up his clothes. For a time all the clothes he had were a T-shirt, Levis, swimming trunks, tennis shoes, and a Robin Hood outfit, all of which we used to put out for the night, like the cat.

Later he acquired a Boy Scout uniform, a pair of hard shoes, and a suit he wore when he visited his grandmother. These, he realized, had to be hung up indoors.

The closet was four feet wide and two feet deep, with sliding doors and two racks—one for garments and one for shoes. We left it temporarily in the living room while he made room for it in the den.

He sold his railroad to a younger boy, making a neat profit on my investment. But he still had the drafting board, the chemical set, the *Complete Works of A. Conan Doyle,* the dogs, the cat, the reptilarium and the scattered pages of a social studies theme entitled *How the Pirates Won the Pennant* by D. F. Smith.

It was some time before these treasures could be settled, leaving room for the closet. In the interim the closet certainly wasn't wasted. I found it a good place to put my golf bag. My wife filled the top shelf with hats that either came from or were destined for a PTA rummage sale, and the cat took over the shoe rack. He wouldn't come out except to eat.

Some weeks later, after all this had been resolved, I paid a call on Douglas. I wanted to see if he had yet given his new room his own personal stamp and essence, transformed it from a vacant cubicle into a storehouse of spiritual riches.

I hoped to find inside this room the echo and imprint of one human being, struggling for identity in the wilderness. I knocked at the door. An act of simple courtesy.

"*Entrez-vous!*" he shouted. We try to speak at least one foreign language every day. I tried the door. Something was against it.

"Wait a minute," he called. "It's the reptilarium."

There was a sound of commotion inside, such as might be made by a weasel wrestling a blacksnake in a corn crib.

The door opened. "You can come in now," he said.

It was a wondrous sight. The room looked as if a capricious tide had rushed through a dime store, collecting flotsam, and deposited its cargo on this unlikely shore.

The impact was stunning. I removed an undershirt, a white football, a sweat sock, a set of Scrabble, and a handwritten composition on the First Continental Congress from a chair and sank into it.

"What's the meaning of this?" I demanded when I could talk.

He looked around innocently. "Of what?"

"This room, man!" I bellowed. "It's a disgrace. A shambles. A disaster."

I swept an arm over the appalling panorama. I kicked out at the cluttered floor. A pamphlet entitled *Salamanders and Newts* skittered away and flapped down on a stiff old canvas water bag.

"What's that desiccated relic for?" I asked.

"In case," he said, "I am ever lost in the desert."

Everything on the floor, I soon discovered, was equally vital. The fractured suitcase, the blackened light globe, the crayon sketch of Crazy Horse in full feather, the colored bubble gum portrait of Bill Mazeroski (a second baseman), the postage stamp from the Falkland Islands, the photograph of the USS *Constitution* in drydock at Boston, the model of the X-15, the mimeographed examination paper beginning, "One yard equals how many inches?"

I waded to the door through the debris.

"I want all of this stuff put back wherever it belongs," I commanded, "before you leave this room."

"Now?"

"Now!" I said. I went out and shut the door, leaving him alone in his temple of solitude with his innermost fancies.

I FOUND A FAIRLY DECENT SATYR

Perhaps home decorating is the great American pastime. From the newlyweds with their paint brushes and homemade mobiles to the Bel-Air *nouveau riche* with their hired decorators, the American couple are forever coloring, hanging, accenting, furnishing and otherwise dabbling with their abodes.

Most people don't know anything about décor, but they know what they like. And the differences in artistic taste between mates who otherwise seem reasonably compatible can be a strain on marriage.

We went out to buy a picture frame one Saturday morning. The boys went with us. They are developing a sense of aesthetics. It was to be an elevating group experience. But it turned out badly.

We saw an ad where a factory was closing out hundreds of frames, of various sizes, at prices so low you had to buy one even if you didn't want a frame.

"We'll pick up something for when we remodel the den," I said. We stopped in a bookshop to look at prints on the way to the frame factory.

"We ought to know what we want the frame for," I explained.

We all set to work thumbing through the catalogues and the racks of mounted prints.

"How about this one?" my wife said. She had turned up *Danseuse sur la scene,* by Degas. "Isn't it lovely?"

"It's lovely, all right," I agreed, "if you like ballet dancers. I prefer something more dynamic."

"How about this, Pa?" asked Curt. He had found the Bellows painting in which Luis Firpo, the bull of the Pampas, is knocking Jack Dempsey through the ropes.

"That was a great moment in ring history," I admitted. "But I wouldn't want it hanging on my wall. It's too dynamic. I'd keep waiting for Dempsey to climb back and poleax that ox."

My wife was standing back from one of Corot's misty green landscapes. "Isn't it relaxing?" she sighed. "I love Corot."

"That's the trouble with Corot," I said. "He's too relaxing. Too bucolic. He always makes me feel like a picnic lunch."

Just then I happened on Renoir's *The Bathers,* that voluptuous canvas in which a clutch of Renoir's hippy nudes are frolicking in the Seine.

"Now this is something more like it!" I exclaimed. "You have the restful bucolic feeling, and yet you also have the dynamism of the human body."

"Don't you think," my wife said, "you ought to buy the frame first? So you'll know what size print to get?"

"I guess that's a good idea," I agreed. I took a parting look at Renoir's sportive *jeunes filles,* and we went to the frame factory. I picked out three frames, one eighteen by twenty, one eighteen by twenty-four and one twenty-four by thirty-six.

"Why three?" my wife asked. "Don't we only need one?"

"Yes, we only need one frame," I explained, "but we don't know what size print we're going to pick out, do we? So we have to get three frames. Then we can be pretty sure one will fit."

"Well, good heavens!" she said. "That seems pretty foolish. Can't you just get one frame and then pick out a print the same size?"

"Are you out of your mind?" I said. "Are you going to let the size of a frame you happen to have, because you got it on sale, determine your taste in art?"

"Well, I'm only trying to say," she said, "why didn't you pick out the print first then?"

"Why didn't I indeed!" I said. I'm afraid I was shouting.

We didn't get any frames or any picture either. Sometimes I think I'm living with a pack of Philistines.

I also think I was euchered out of that Renoir.

We had lived in our house ten years before I realized my wife was deliberately furnishing the living room in blond. I might never have found out, if the television set hadn't broken down.

The television man drove up for a look at it. He shook his head, my wife told me later, and explained to her how the manifold might be all right, though it was most unlikely, and in any case, the thing the voltage passes through, or whatever, was the wrong kind and never belonged in this particular set anyway, but the real danger was the excellent probability that the picture tube was blown.

"Anyway," she added, "if it isn't, he said it will be before long. He said it's a miracle it's lasted as long as it has—if it really has—which he doubts."

"What'd he suggest?" I asked. I'm not an expert on the jargon of the electronic world.

"He said he'd take it on a trade. He has a blond one for sale."

"A blond one what?" I asked. I hadn't, up to that moment, associated blond with furniture.

"A blond television. Blond wood. The one we have is mahogany, you know. It's never matched our décor."

"I didn't know we had a décor," I said. "What is it, anyway?"

"Well, I suppose you'd call it a blond Swedish modern."

It had never occurred to me. When we got our furniture after the war it was a pottage of heirlooms, white elephants, painted packing crates, and a quaint living room group that I would call Calvin Coolidge Spanish.

"How did we happen to wind up with all this blond Swedish modern?" I asked.

Through the years, she explained, as one of our old pieces after another sank to its knees and was thrown out to die, it was replaced by a new one. Each new piece was selected more or less to match the last new piece. In this way, gradually, the entire nondescript mess had been replaced by this modern Swedish blond mess.

"How did we happen to start out on blond?" I asked.

"It was when I got the record cabinet," she said, "with green stamps. The only one they had was blond."

It's odd how a man's whole environment can hinge on a seemingly minor happenstance such as that.

"How come, then," I said, "if we were on this blond kick, we bought a mahogany TV?"

"We didn't buy it. Your mother gave it to us. Remember? You said you would never buy one, never. And she bought one because she said she didn't want the boys to grow up illiterate."

"Well, if my mother gave it to us," I said, "I don't think we ought to trade it off. Why don't we just keep it and start out in reverse—replace all this blond Swedish modern stuff one at a time until everything is mahogany?"

She went out to the kitchen and slammed the door lightly and began cooking something. Women cook things as an outlet for their hostilities.

I never realized she felt that strongly about mahogany.

She also went through a beige phase that was difficult. It was right after we all went to the Interior Decorator's Show. Everybody came home in a fever. We were all like Michelangelo contemplating the bare ceiling of the Sistine Chapel. Something noble had to be done.

"I'd like to paint the living room over," my wife said. She put her index finger against pursed lips and narrowed her eyes the way women do when they are getting ready to tear a house apart.

"What color this time?" I asked. The living room had already been light green, dark green, light beige, dark beige, and something called Samarkand.

"A kind of beige, I think," she said.

"It's already a kind of beige, isn't it?" I asked.

"It's too cold," she explained. "I'd like a slightly warmer beige."

Women have some mystic way of classifying colors by their heat.

She said she would also like to get a new console table because ours was too short, too low, too narrow, out of style, and the wrong color of beige.

"I don't see that it makes any difference," I said. "You can't see it anyway for all the junk on it. You could paint it a hot purple and nobody would ever suspect."

I reminded her about the time I lost my eyeglasses on it for a week and missed out on the last chapter of an Erle Stanley Gardner serial in the *Post*.

They might never have turned up except one of the boys was looking for his roller skates on the table and found my eyeglasses under an old raincoat. They had fallen somehow into a tennis shoe.

There was also some conflict over my French poster. I glued it on the living room wall next to the louver doors that open into the den. When you turn the lights down and squeeze your eyes up you can easily imagine it is the entrance to a cafe on the Place Pigalle. It is very warm.

"It looks like a set for the *Folies Bergère*," my wife said.

"That's very flattering," I said, "but I don't think it's really that good. I don't pretend to be an interior decorator. It's just that I know what I like."

Even the boys were eager to take down their airline calendars and do their own walls over in tasteful beauty.

"I'd like to have a real good oil painting, Pa," said Doug.

"That's fine, my boy," I said. "Which one?"

"*Custer's Last Stand*," he said.

I was gratified, of course, by the lad's splendid taste. But if anybody was to have *Custer's Last Stand* for his room, it would be me, I told him. I had lusted after that magnificent canvas ever since my father took me into my first saloon and bought me a pickled egg.

For the moment, however, I had other plans.

"My thought," I told my wife, "is to glue my Spanish bullfighting poster to the inside of the front door. Then when I turn the lights down I can easily imagine I'm in Seville, with the great Manolete about to enter the ring. It will be very warm."

She said if I tried anything like that she would hide the glue.

My own taste has always run to marble. Once a man has climbed the noble slopes of the Acropolis and contemplated the beautiful geometry of the Parthenon he can never again be content with plastic.

And among the great stones of the classic world, travertine has always been my favorite. It may not have the ice of green serpentine, nor the fire of the *breche rose*. But it has warmth and serenity and character.

Travertine was the substance of the Colosseum, Saint Peter's, and half the palazzos of Rome. It has endured the centuries with dignity.

I never expected, of course, to dwell in marble halls. All I ever hoped for was to own a cocktail table with a travertine top.

And now, at long last, I do.

This treasure did not come into my household without hardship and sacrifice.

I first saw my travertine table—although I didn't know then that it was to be mine—in a junk shop window. The shop was closed for the night. In the street light the window was a jumble of dusty shadows.

But my wife spied the table. She has a keen eye for the merely worthless among the false and tawdry in a junk shop.

"Look!" she cried. "A travertine table."

It was travertine indeed—but past its glory. It rested on a base which, weary with many years, sagged in the middle. My travertine had sagged with it. It was cracked in two.

"Yes," I said sadly. "A noble stone, nobly cracked."

"I bet I could get it for next to nothing," she whispered, as if some sharp competitor might overhear.

"It's no use," I told her. "I'm afraid this one is beyond help. It hasn't endured the centuries with dignity."

"Oh, well," she said. "You'll get your travertine some day."

"Perhaps," I said, "it will come posthumously."

I should have sensed something was up. She didn't look back at the junk shop, but in her eye there was the fire of *breche rose*.

I forgot the incident. Then one morning when I got up I found the table in the living room. The cracked section was missing. The travertine was now in two equal parts.

"Well," she said. "What do you think?"

"How'd you ever saw it in two?" I asked.

"We took it to a stonemason's. Where they make tombstones. He only charged me three dollars."

"They wanted to carve your name on it for five dollars more, Pa," said Curt. "Ma wouldn't go for it."

"I should think not," I said. "A bit too showy, that."

"Guess how much I got the table for?" she said.

I figured the junk store man would have sensed her emotional need for the table and swindled her. Even then, he shouldn't have dared to ask more than eight or ten dollars.

"Fifteen dollars," I said gallantly.

"Only twelve," she said. "You think I was crazy?"

"Certainly not," I said. "It has warmth. Serenity. Character."

We were content until the Daltons asked us over one night for Irish mists. They had a new travertine table. I knew my wife was ill with curiosity, but would never ask what it cost.

"Ah, travertine, I believe!" I said casually. I ran a hand over the smooth translucent surface. "I'm very fond of it, you know. It has dignity, serenity."

"Oh, that," said Dalton. "I picked it up at an auction. Guess what I paid for it?"

"Seventy dollars?" I guessed. "Eighty?"

"Ten bucks."

I glanced at my wife. Her eyes had the ice of green serpentine.

"It's a fine piece," I told Dalton. "But you ought to have it sawed in half. Takes the strain off the middle, you know."

So at last I had my travertine. But still my brightest dream was unfulfilled. *A statue in the yard.* I'd wanted my own statue since that shining day as a youth when I first looked upon the gleaming marbles in the gardens of the late railroad magnate, Mr. Henry E. Huntington.

I had the birdbath of course; a wretched thing, but my own. Sometimes in summer twilight, when the sprinklers were going on the lawn and the air was laced with iridescent beads of water, it was no trick to see the birdbath as a fountain. But in the morning it was only a birdbath.

My hunger would never be satisfied by some concrete reindeer or goose or any of those Disneyland creatures so cherished by those who have never looked on beauty rare. No, I must have a statue in the heroic mold—the Emperor Marcus Aurelius astride his bronze horse; Laocoön and his sons entwined in eternal struggle with the reptiles; the goddess Aphrodite rising from the sea.

I meant to place it on the ivy-grown hillock among the three pine trees, where it would seem to live in a grotto of ever-changing light and shadow. It would be mostly shielded from the neighbors, who would merely add it to my catalogue of supposed eccentricities.

But I could lie on the chaise longue in the patio and enjoy it privately, like a pagan alone in a temple before a graven god.

I nearly got my statue once, but something went wrong.

I had hinted around to a man who worked for a certain cemetery much given to the display of statuary. I did not want a perfect statue, I explained to this fellow, but only something which the cemetery, for one reason or another, had discarded.

"It might be Michelangelo's *David*," I explained, "or *Perseus with the Head of Medusa*—with maybe a thumb broken off, or some other appendage, which would make it unsuitable for the cemetery but wouldn't bother me in the least."

There must be some such treasure lying around, rejected, in the cemetery's storehouse, I suggested. It was two or three years after I first broached the subject that my friend told me he had come up with something.

He held a party in my honor, in the course of which he presented me with a little statue he had made himself out of plaster of Paris. It was only a token, he said, of the full-size statue he had managed to obtain for me.

This, he disclosed, was a copy of Rodin's *The Kiss*, which, he explained, had been considered perhaps a bit too voluptuous for the cemetery's purposes.

"You aren't just whistling in the dark!" I exclaimed, genuinely impressed. "That might even be too racy for *my* back yard."

He had also arranged for one of his employer's ground crews to deliver the statue in a truck and imbed it in concrete in my yard that very night, during the party.

I could hardly wait until an hour when I could decently leave the party and rush home to see my statue for the first time by moonlight. But there was no statue; only the old birdbath, rough-hewn and askew.

My friend felt he may have erred in rewarding the workers in advance with a bottle of spirits and that they may have become befuddled and imbedded the Rodin in the wrong yard.

That was five or six years ago. Ever since that night, whenever I'm driving around town, I keep my eye peeled for *The Kiss* adorning the yard of some accidental beneficiary. But that thrill has never come.

In desperation one Sunday I drove out to a statue dealer's, tremulous but drawn on as if to some shrine, the way a man goes out to look at new cars.

I'm glad I don't own a cemetery. Buying statuary is not a happy business. It is fraught with conflicts of morals as well as aesthetics and finances. One must make decisions of the utmost delicacy.

I left my wife at home. I was afraid I might be influenced by her taste. It runs to cherubs, fawns, and flamingos standing on one leg.

I drove out toward Beverly Hills and found a place that seemed to have a statue for everyone. I was waited on by a young lady with a figure that put me in mind of Houdon's *Diana*.

"I'm looking," I told her, "for a statue to go in the back yard, by the patio."

I explained that it ought to please the eye as well as elevate the spirit.

"You want an angel?" she asked.

"Oh, no, not that," I said. "An angel might be considered out of place by some of the neighbors."

I could just hear Dalton on the phone if he ever looked through his spyglass and saw an angel in my yard.

"Maybe an Aphrodite," I said, "rising from the sea."

She looked around. "I don't think we have an Aphrodite today. What about a David?"

She showed me a small Michelangelo's *David*. It had a fig leaf which didn't appear to be Michelangelo's work.

"Do you have it," I asked, "without the uh, leaf?"

"Not at the moment," she said, "but we have some on order. Everybody wants it without the leaf. They feel nothing should be added that wasn't put there by the artist himself."

"I agree," I said. "However, I'm not sure I'd want a David anyway.

His expression is a little too stern, don't you think? I mean, for a patio and all?"

"What about a nice satyr?" the young lady suggested.

"No," I said, "I'm not too strong for the cloven hoof. Do you have anything in a wood nymph? Or a sprite?"

"We have a lovely Venus," she said, leading me to a figure of a supple maid holding a round fruit in her hand.

"Is that an apple," I asked, "or a pomegranate?"

"I really don't know," said the salesgirl. "Maybe it's a quince."

I liked the Venus. She seemed to symbolize voluptuousness and modesty, innocence and promise, restraint and abandon—all the qualities that ideally reside in woman. I thought she might give the patio exactly the touch it needed.

It turned out the Venus wasn't for sale. She was only a prototype, from whose mold others were to be cast.

"Well," my wife said when I got home. "Where've you been?"

"Oh, shopping around," I said.

"See anything interesting?"

"Not much," I said. "I found a fairly decent satyr. And a Venus I rather liked. But what I really had in mind was a nymph. Or a sprite."

She sighed. "I was hoping," she said, "we could make the Dodge do for another year."

It might have been simpler just to go ahead and get a one-legged flamingo.

GET THOSE MONSTERS OUT OF THE DEN

Sinister things began to happen around our house not long after we bought Doug the microscope for his birthday. I assumed he would have many happy hours with this instrument in the study of leaves and petals and maybe insect wings.

I detected the change that was creeping over him one night when I got home from work and started our usual roundup of the day's major league baseball games.

"The Dodgers beat the Giants six to three," I told him.

"Um-hm," he said. He was bent over the microscope.

"I think," I said, "it was a matter of good pitching and bold base running, mostly."

"I think I've got a *paramecium* here," he said. "Come and take a look."

I went over and peered through his microscope. I don't know what he had, but it looked to me like one of those Japanese one-man submarines at Pearl Harbor.

"Where'd you get that?" I asked.

"Miss Clatter gave it to me," he said. "It was dehydrated. When you put it in water it comes back to life. Watch. I'm going to feed him."

"Feed him? Feed him what? I'm feeding enough animals around here already."

"It's something Miss Clatter gave us," he said. "When they eat it they turn blue. It makes them easier to see."

"I know what you mean," I said. "I ate something in Naples once that made me turn blue."

The *paramecium* ate the food and turned blue. He looked like a blue one-man submarine.

"They're not nearly as interesting, though," he said, "as the *vorticella*."

"What's that?"

"The *vorticella*," he explained, "has a long twisting tail and a huge mouth. They jump at their food and devour it in one gulp and run away."

"I see," I said. "Something like a teen-ager."

"Other one-celled animals," he explained, "eat by casually drifting over their food in an amorphous mass and absorbing it."

"Sounds like a Rotary Club luncheon," I said. "Where'd you find these *vorticella*, anyway?"

"Right here at home," he said. "I scraped them off of Mama's plant in the vase on the bookcase. Miss Clatter was amazed."

"You mean they're rare?"

"Miss Clatter says ours is the only house she ever heard of in her career that produced a *vorticella*."

From then on I knew we were living in the twilight zone. I believe the human eye sometimes pries into secrets it was never meant to see.

The house had become a laboratory. The mechanical eye of the microscope had discovered the subliminal world about us. Our placid sanctuary was in reality a jungle in which the most primitive blobs of organic matter were waging a cannibalistic struggle for survival.

Even our supposedly antiseptic kitchen was exposed as a primeval breeding ground. We saw things we never wished to see.

One evening young Pasteur called me over to his work table to examine something he had in focus. I squinted into the eyepiece. What I saw squirming in the light looked like a transparent fountain pen with a plastic gizzard and two tails. It was thrashing around like a belly dancer.

"Good Lord!" I whispered. "What's that?"

"I'm not sure, Pa," he said. "It's either a *rotifer* or a *rhizopod*, unless it's an *amoeba*."

"Where did you find him?" I demanded.

"In the flower bowl on the cocktail table. There's millions there. They divide like crazy."

I summoned my wife. "Do you know," I said, "that your flower bowl is a dividing place for millions of foul microbes?"

She threw out the chrysanthemums and the teeming water and washed the bowl.

"It won't do any good, Ma," said Doug. "They'll be back. They drop down in the dust. Like paratroopers."

Later on I found a damp heel of bread in a saucer on the sink.

"This bread," I told my wife, "appears to be moldy." I detest mold.

"I know," she said. "The mad scientist is growing something."

"Growing something? What are we running around here. A swamp?"

"It's an experiment, Pa," Doug said. "I'm on the trail of a wonder drug."

He also disclosed that he was keeping a bowl of tap water in a pitcher on the bookcase.

"It's aging," he explained.

It seems that tap water is no good for research because it's full of chlorine. Everything alive in it is dead. He had to age it until the chlorine wore out. Then it was fit to grow microbes in.

Our experience with one-celled animals hardly conditioned us for the next stage in the lad's career in pathology. I first found out about this hideous development one evening when I heard a faint crackling in the house, like paper being crumpled and torn. It seemed to be emanating from my den, which by this time had been converted into a laboratory.

"What's that?" I whispered, cocking an ear.

Doug's face reflected acute distress.

"What is it?" I demanded. "What have you got in there?"

"It's my guinea pigs, Pa," he said.

"Your what? Guinea pigs?"

"They're my term project," he said. "In life science. They're in a box lined with newspapers. They keep chewing up the newspapers."

"Get those monsters out of the den," I commanded in as calm a voice as I could manage. "I'm not having any idiot rodents in my den."

"Don't worry," he said. "I'm building them a cage."

"What are you going to do with guinea pigs, anyway?" I demanded. "Just observe them?"

He folded his arms and looked me in the eye. "I'm going to dissect them, Pa. I'm going to do my term report on the anatomy of the guinea pig."

"*Dissect* them!" I cried. "Over my dead body!"

I was perturbed. I'd always thought of him as compassionate toward the lower species, like St. Francis of the Animals.

"It's your own fault, in a way," my wife said. "You urged him to see *The Young Doctors*. You said it might inspire him."

"It did, too," he said. "I'm going to be a pathologist."

"A pathologist!" I said. "Why can't you be something more romantic? A psychiatrist. A chiropodist."

"The hero of *The Young Doctors* was a pathologist," my wife said. "So was Fredric March. He was wonderful. He should have won an Academy Award."

"Good Lord!" I groaned. "I suppose that makes sense. Just because Fredric March ought to get an Oscar, my son is going to become a pathologist. I told him *The Hustler* was a good movie, too. You think I want him to play pool for a living?"

In my anguish I leaped up and bumped against the bookcase. A coffee can crashed to the floor. Doug got down on his knees and looked sadly into the rubble on the rug.

"Pa," he said, "you've knocked over my larva."

"I'm sorry," I said. "I'm really very sorry. What kind of a larva was it?" I asked. I don't like to destroy any live thing.

"I'm not sure," he said. "It might have been a butterfly."

I sank into my chair. What a wretched day. My home had been turned into an abattoir and I had been responsible for the destruction of a potential butterfly.

A few days later I accidentally came across the application for the body of a dead cat.

People who say they dislike cats, I've found out, are almost psychopathically hated by large numbers of people who love cats.

But I can't help my feelings. It isn't that I dislike cats. It's that I'm uncomfortable around a cat. And when a cat is around me, he's uncomfortable. He or she. That's one of the troubles. I can never tell what sex a cat is. Being around somebody whose sex I don't know always makes me uncomfortable.

If there's anything that makes me more uncomfortable to be around than a live cat, it is a cat that has passed on.

You may understand, then, my dismay when I discovered this horrifying document. I happened to find it crumpled in a ball on the living room floor and picked it up out of curiosity.

It read like this, with the names changed, of course, for the comfort of all concerned:

> *Dear Mrs. Frobisher:*
>
> *I'm a student at Benjamin Franklin High School. For a science project I will need a freshly disposed of cat. I was told to write you for authorization to get one. Will you please send a note to the animal shelter giving them permission to let me take a cat? I have enclosed a request for the cat from my biology instructor.*

I didn't have to inquire who had composed this ghastly epistle. It was obviously my younger son, inspired undoubtedly by his morbid ambition to become an autopsy surgeon.

"What," I asked my wife, "does the monster plan to do with this deceased specimen? Or do I know all too well?"

"I suppose," she said, "he intends to dissect it."

I shuddered. "Not in this house."

"You told him," she said, "he could do whatever he wanted in the garage, so long as you didn't know about it."

"Good God," I sighed. "I won't even dare park the car."

In my anguish I leaped up and bumped against the bookcase. A small bottle crashed to the floor. Doug dashed from his room.

"Pa!" he cried. "You've knocked my *naiads* over!"

"Naiads!" I croaked. "What are *naiads?*"

"They're water larvas," he said.

"Larvae," I said. "If you're going to be a pathologist you have to know your Latin plurals. Also, what do you mean by 'a freshly disposed of cat'?"

"What's wrong with that?" he asked cautiously.

"Don't you think it should be 'a cat that has been disposed of'?"

"Isn't that ending a sentence with a preposition?" he said.

He was right, of course. But I wondered which was the greater sin, ending a sentence with a preposition or ending a cat with a dissection.

I will say the lad's passion for science has made him an inspiring figure for some of the younger children in the neighborhood. Victoria, the little girl next door, was herself enflamed for a time. She decided she wanted to be Madame Curie, instead of Tuesday Weld.

She explained this when she came over to borrow a spoonful of hops. She had been borrowing odd things lately. Last time it was a pinch of ginger.

"I don't have any hops," I told her. "How about a nice, cold root beer?"

"No," she said, "I have to have the hops. I need it for the ambrosia."

"Good Lord, Victoria!" I exclaimed. "What are you cooking?"

"It's not cooking," she said. "It's chemistry. I'm going to be a scientist. The nation needs women's brains."

"Well, yes," I agreed. "We could use more women's brains, all right. What kind of a scientist are you going to be?"

"I'm going to make an elixir," said Victoria, "that will make everybody beautiful and happy. Like ambrosia, you know, that the Greek gods and goddesses drank? They were the most beautiful people in all of history."

"I guess they were beautiful, all right," I granted, "but they weren't always terribly happy. They had plenty of troubles."

"I didn't know that," said Victoria. "Goodbye."

She walked pensively away.

Later Doug came in and got his chemistry set. He said he was going to Victoria's to help her out.

"What are you people up to anyway?" I asked.

"She just wants to pick my brain, Pa," he said. "She doesn't really know what she's doing."

"Well, what *is* she doing?" I demanded.

"Beats me," he said. "She says she's making ambrosia. Says it makes everybody happy like the Greeks."

"What has she put in it so far?"

"She hasn't mixed it up yet. She's just getting her ingredients together. Powdered clay, charcoal, cat vitamins, hair bleach, and some rubber eraser filings that come off the eraser, you know, when you erase something."

"That ought to make the gods happy," I said. "Don't tell me she's actually going to mix that stuff all up!"

"Don't worry, Pa," he said. "Nothing will happen. She hasn't got any catalyst."

All the same, I was uneasy until they both came back. They were sound of limb. They said they had come after the baseball bat. They looked beautiful and happy.

"How's the old elixir coming, Victoria?" I asked.

"My mother won't let me make it," she said. "She says it's the witch's brew. She says she doesn't want me to be a chemist. They are mostly hermits and have brown fingernails. I might be a space woman."

"There will always be room for beautiful girls with brains," I assured her. "Even in space."

She nodded sagely. "Mr. Smith," she said, "do you still have that root beer?"

It was Thoreau that finally lured Doug away from the laboratory and into the fresh air.

I was happy to see the change, although something has happened to Thoreau since I was a boy. His song of the simple life in the wilderness no longer stirs my blood. I realize I've been corrupted by our material prosperity. I suppose I could never go back.

Through Doug, though, I've been re-exposed to overpowering draughts of Thoreau. Walden has become his Bible, the outdoors his temple, and nature his faith.

His baptism in Walden Pond has tainted his thinking. We are philosophically estranged. He is no longer the all-American, capitalist-oriented product of the affluent society that I tried to make him.

As far as I can tell from listening, the basic discipline of his new view of life is the renunciation of material things.

"I'm all for that," I told him. "I'd like to see some others around here get over the idea that human fulfillment can be bought in the supermarket."

"Thoreau says," he pointed out, "that most people don't really live in their houses—they're prisoners in them."

"That's nonsense," I said. "After all, one of man's earliest impulses was to provide shelter for his family."

"Thoreau says," he went on, "that most people don't own their houses—their houses own them."

"Times are different," I assured him. "Thoreau never heard of the FHA. Besides, how would you like to live in a tent?"

"It's okay with me," he said.

He went into the kitchen. I could tell what he was doing by the sounds. He opened the electric icebox. He opened a can of something with the electric can opener. Tuna, I guessed. He toasted some bread in the electric toaster. He opened the icebox. He opened a can of something. That stumped me. He mixed something in the electric blender. Of course. Frozen orange juice.

He came back, eating a toasted tuna sandwich, with mayonnaise and pickle, and drinking a glass of foamy orange juice.

"You see, Pa," he explained, talking with his mouth full, "Thoreau says a man ought to build his house with his hands, the way a bird does, and have a simple diet, like an animal."

"What does he say about modern inventions," I asked, "like, say, kitchen appliances?"

He chewed reflectively on his tuna sandwich. "Thoreau says," he went on, "that most modern improvements are an illusion. About the only implements he needed were a knife, an ax, a spade, and a wheelbarrow."

He went back into the kitchen. "Be sure," I reminded him, "to wash up your dishes."

"I will," he said. I could hear him splashing at the sink. "I'll sure be glad," he called out, "when you get Ma that dishwasher you keep talking about."

I didn't pay any attention. I was wondering if I could make a tuna sandwich with an ax and a wheelbarrow.

WHERE DID YOU PUT THE CORKSCREW?

We have to escape now and then from the megalopolis. One weekend we borrowed Magruder's Volkswagen camper and drove to the Colorado River.

I have always loved the desert, in all its moods. That day it chose to be sullen. We drove from Barstow to Needles through a sandstorm. Sand lifted from the desert in clouds and funnels, as water rises in storms at sea.

It pushed and pelted us. It drew stripes on the highway and daubed the sky beige. It played shrill tunes in our windows.

At the wheel, in the bubble of the cockpit, I felt like a pilot taking a Piper Cub through from Bagdad to Samarra on a mission of the utmost importance to world peace.

"You think we should turn back?" my wife shouted. She was in back on the bunk.

"Never," I said through gritty teeth.

The Amboy crater emerged from the gloom on the horizon off the starboard bow, a dead volcano entombed in eternal silence amid the cold black debris of its primeval rages. In this eerie light it seemed alive and malevolent.

The sun burned red through the angry sky. Half a moon hung cockeyed above a spiney mountain. Grotesque trees and cacti writhed in the wind. I would not have been surprised if a pterodactyl had flapped into our windshield.

"Black lava!" It was a joyous shout from aft. "Can't we stop and get a few rocks?"

She had been after me for years to get her some black lava for the cactus garden. I could not picture myself out on that wind-raked sea of frozen black foam, harvesting rocks for a woman's whim.

"No can do," I said.

"Why not?"

"Because of Pele," I said. "Him volcano god. Him angry when white man steal lava."

"Don't be silly," she said. "Besides, isn't Pele the Hawaiian volcano god? The one they had in Hawaii when we were there?"

"No matter," I explained. "Hawaii all a same state now. Him got jurisdiction Mojave Desert."

"Why don't we stop?" she insisted.

"Because," I said, dropping the pidgin English as fruitless, "it's against the law to take lava out of season. It's protected, like buffalo."

That seemed to satisfy her. She's very law abiding for a woman.

In Needles we stopped at an oasis and had a half-gallon pitcher full of cold root beer in icy mugs. I felt like Lawrence of Arabia.

From Needles we drove down along the river toward Blythe and found a river campsite somewhere in the dark.

The road from Needles to Blythe is one of the few lonely roads left in California, perhaps in the world.

It winds and dips through cactus, scrawny trees, and forests of ocotillo, that aristocrat of the southwestern desert. The mountains lie low on the edges of the Colorado Valley, as sinister as preying reptiles.

Now and then a desert rodent scuttles across the road, tail high. The river rushes silently into view through a break in the brush, then vanishes again.

We scared an eagle from a dry tree beside the road. He beat his wings and climbed the sky, raking us with an evil yellow eye and dragging his awesome shadow across our windshield.

"Did you see that!" shouted Doug. "It must have been a vulture!"

"It was an eagle," I said calmly. I was trying to get the camper back on the road.

"It was a hawk, Pa," said Curt.

"It was an eagle," I said.

"Are you sure it wasn't a crow?" said my wife.

"Good Lord!" I muttered in disgust. "A crow!"

"Have you ever seen an eagle before?" she said.

"Hundreds."

"Where?"

"On the back of a silver dollar, of course."

She laughed. "You mean an eagle on a *coin?*"

"An eagle," I explained, "is an eagle."

Dark fell with the suddenness of a window blind. I felt a stab of foreboding. There was no light but a faint glow from a fragment of the moon and the beams of our headlights.

We turned down toward the river at a sign pointing to a trailer camp. We took a cabin for ourselves and put the camper under the trees where the boys made camp.

In the dark, with a desert wind assaulting us at thirty knots, we built a charcoal fire in our hibachi and cooked wieners and a can of pork and beans. It was indescribably delicious.

I dug in our stores for the bottle of Burgundy I had stowed away the previous night with such admirable foresight. This was the supreme moment of the day.

"Where's the corkscrew?" I asked, turning the cool bottle lovingly in my hands.

There was a silence, an ominous silence.

"Where did you put the corkscrew?" I repeated. "The corkscrew, for the Burgundy?"

"I'm afraid," she said, "I didn't think to pack one."

As I picked away at the cork with Curt's pocket knife, taking care not to push the cork into the wine or cut off a finger, I reflected on the common truth that few artifacts on which civilized man depends are as indispensable as the corkscrew. Not even the match.

In the morning, we went down to the river to watch the sun come up over Arizona. It was inspiring, but chilly.

"Boy," I said, "that first cup of coffee's going to taste good. Where is the coffee, anyway?"

There was an ominous silence.

That moment came back to me some weeks later when Douglas and I set out alone for Death Valley. The others elected to stay behind that weekend for reasons now forgotten.

I suppose it is some streak of atavism in the city man that makes him seek out such desolation as that of Death Valley. American civilization has ground most of its wilderness underfoot, but here is a landscape that still awes the traveler with its malignant beauty.

The bulldozer, the concrete mixer and the water engineer have done little to reform this stubborn outback.

From Zabriskie Point, the view can be little different from that which shriveled the souls of the forty-niners.

The valley stretches out in reptilian stillness at the foot of tumultuous mountains. Even in a good car on good roads, one descends with a sense of foreboding.

We drove for miles in silence past the dead lakes of salt, where absolutely nothing grows and nothing crawls. It is a scene that silences a human being.

At a place called Bad Water, which is a euphemism, a poison pool lies blinking in its bed of salt like a snake's eye, marking the lowest point in the United States.

Peering into this sump, one can easily believe that the distillate of all the world's evil is puddled here.

We stopped at Furnace Creek Ranch for gas.

"We're going on to Scotty's Castle," I told the gas man. "Can we get gas up there?"

"There ain't no place you can't get gas," he said in what I took to be a taciturn indictment of civilization.

We stopped at the sand dunes and walked into them until we were lost in a world of sand and sky. There was no life but our own thumping hearts.

We found a thread of infinitesimal footprints, like stitchwork in the perfect surface of the sand.

"Insect tracks," said my son, who is a naturalist.

I wondered if the insect was aware, as it dragged itself over the sand, inch by silent inch, that it wasn't going anywhere; that its route was hopeless; its destination indistinguishable from its starting place. Insects, of course, don't have man's omniscience.

We turned into Grapevine Canyon and found the Castle. I was surprised to find the parking area crowded. People were shopping for souvenirs or eating at the sandwich bar or waiting for the hourly tour.

We didn't take the tour. I am sure Scotty didn't take the Castle seriously. It does not, as sometimes suggested, symbolize a man's triumph over Death Valley, but his defeat. Somehow this cakelike architectural jest seems more comic than elegant in the midst of such natural majesty.

A cross marks Scotty's grave on a hill above the bell tower, and one can fancy hearing his sly laughter rippling down the forlorn wind off the Funeral Mountains.

There is a plaque up there with Scotty's credo:

> *I got four things to live by. Don't say nothing that will hurt anybody. Don't give advice—nobody will take it anyway. Don't complain and don't explain.*

It is a philosophy worth driving through Death Valley to read.

We went into the sandwich bar and had a hamburger. There ain't no place you can't get a hamburger.

That night we camped in a wash known as Mesquite Canyon, a few miles below the Castle.

It was to be a harrowing night, a night fraught with such suffering and misadventure as those that beset the forty-niners and gave the valley its macabre name.

Its beginning was routine, even pleasant. The sun was down behind the Panamints when we descended to our campsite in this scrawny grove of mesquite and cottonwood trees.

Doug struck out in the dusk to take a hike on the Venusian landscape while I made camp. There was a settlement of tents and trailers up by the spring. But we were far out on the edge, alone.

I set out the two army cots. We had no tent. We wanted to sleep in the open, under the moon. I should say Doug did. I wanted to sleep in Scotty's Castle.

I set out the hibachi and laid in the charcoal briquettes and got a fire going for our dinner. Daylight faded, but the moon was up, and almost full. It seemed night, yet everything was quite visible, the way it is in movie scenes that are supposed to be outdoors at night.

The charcoal was aglow when Doug came back, his face and clothes moon colored. "Man, this is real Paladin country," he said. "What's for dinner?"

We cooked pork and beans in the can; we spitted wieners on mesquite twigs and boiled tamales in a pot. It seemed not too unlike the kind of dinner a forty-niner might have had, before his provisions ran out.

Doug, it turned out, had forgotten his personal utensils. We laughed about it and shared mine.

"Don't worry," I told him. "Remember how your mother forgot to pack coffee and a corkscrew when we went to the Colorado River?"

He didn't laugh. We fell silent, tangled in our separate thoughts.

"There's something else I forgot, Pa," he said at last. "The sleeping bags."

I choked on a spoonful of beans. "Good Lord!" I exclaimed. "We'll die!"

In an instant the moonlight turned cold. I felt a knife in the balmy air. The misshapen trees and the stony landscape seemed carved of ice.

"Death Valley at night," I said to myself, "without a sleeping bag!"

"Well, I'm turning in," Doug said later. "Good night." He stretched out on his cot, pulled his red ski cap down over his eyes and ears and fell softly asleep. Youth.

I couldn't sleep. I remembered a Jack London story, where a man froze to death in Alaska. I got up and put on my hooded sweatshirt, over my shirt, then my windbreaker, then my sweater. I pulled the hood over my head and lay down again.

I must have dozed. I dreamed of a World War II story I had read about a Norwegian who lay for thirty days in a grave of ice, hiding from the Nazis. I got up. I opened the suitcase and got out all the extra pants, shirts, towels, and undershirts and spread them out over the cot, for insulation.

When my back grew cold, I turned my chest to the wind, and vice versa, like something being frozen on a spit. Somewhere in the desolate night a coyote laughed.

When I woke up, Doug was frying eggs and whistling.

"Hi, Pa," he called out. "I think you forgot the salt."

I KNEW IT WAS ZACHARY SOMETHING

I was supposed to meet my wife at two forty-five one afternoon at the southeast corner of Sixth and Broadway. We never made it. There was a failure of communications.

In the skills of verbal communications and the giving and receiving of geographical directions, women are enchantingly incompetent.

I speak, of course, of the average woman; the lovable female who enamels her toenails, weeps at Bette Davis movies and can whip up a spinach soufflé on twenty-four hours' notice.

We tried to arrange our meeting by telephone, which is a useful and ingenious instrument but treacherous in communications between man and woman.

"I'll meet you at a quarter to three," I told her, "on the southeast corner of Sixth and Broadway. Try to be on time."

I hung up. She called right back.

"Why did you hang up like that?"

"I thought we were finished," I said. "I told you to meet me on the southeast corner of Sixth and Broadway at two forty-five."

"You said three o'clock."

"No, I actually said a quarter to three."

"Well, that's not the same as two forty-five. I mean, it doesn't *sound* the same even if it is."

"All right," I said, "make it three o'clock. That's a good round time."

"That's too late. We'll be late for the bank."

"All right, then. Make it two forty-five."

"Okay," she said. "A quarter to three, then. By the drugstore."

"What are you talking about—a drugstore? I said on the southeast corner."

"I thought that was the drugstore. Or do you mean the little cafe where we had the Welsh rabbit? It's catty-cornered from the drugstore."

I decided to try a new approach. "Listen. Do you know which way is south?"

"Yes, certainly. It's between the garage and the *Parkinsonia aculeata*. The one with the little yellow flowers the bumblebees eat."

"Fine. Excellent. Now which way is west?"

"You said east before. West is the jewelry shop where you got your watch fixed. Is it working all right?"

"It's running a little fast," I said. "So which way is east?"

"It's the front porch because the sun sets in the patio."

"Wonderful. So you meet me on the corner opposite where the sun sets and between the garage and the whatever kind of tree it is with the yellow flowers the bumblebees eat."

"Come to think of it," she said, "the cafe with the Welsh rabbit was at Seventh. Didn't you say Sixth? Or is that another cafe?"

"Let's start all over," I sighed. "Just get on a bus and put yourself in the hands of the bus driver."

"I just happened to think," she said. "The bank stays open till six on Fridays, doesn't it? I could meet you at three, after all, and we wouldn't get mixed up."

"*Friday?*" I said. "I thought we were talking about today."

"Isn't this Friday?"

"Today is Thursday," I said, "tomorrow is Friday, and on *ad infinitum.*"

"That must be right," she agreed, "because Saturday I have a swimming lesson and that isn't until the day after tomorrow."

"Good," I said. "I'll see you at the watch shop then. At three."

"Well, if today is Thursday," she said, "I can't make it. Hazel Mae is coming over. We're going to cut out patterns."

As it turned out, Thursday was a dead loss. Hazel Mae never got over to cut out patterns. She thought she was supposed to come on Tuesday.

It may be that human affairs have become too complex for ordinary language. We will have to invent some kind of machine to communicate our ideas for us, or else develop extrasensory perception.

I have often thought what a boon it would be to a man if his wife could know what he wanted for dinner through extrasensory perception, instead of having to find out by telephone.

It would eliminate much misunderstanding and perhaps a few divorces. One afternoon about four o'clock, for example, I was unaccountably seized by a yearning for baked pork chops. I phoned home.

"How about baked pork chops for dinner?" I asked my wife.

"What time is it?" she answered, if that may be called an answer.

"Four o'clock. Why?"

"I didn't realize it was that late. What would you like for dinner?"

"How about baked pork chops?"

"Tonight?"

"Yes, tonight. Why not?"

"I was going to have them tomorrow."

"All right, fine. Tomorrow."

"No. We can have them tonight, if you'd rather."

"No, tomorrow will be fine."

"I was going to have veal tonight but we can have that Wednesday night instead."

"Instead of what?"

"Instead of the meatballs. I was going to have the meatballs Wednesday if we had the pork chops tomorrow. But if we have the pork chops tonight I'll have the veal Wednesday instead of the meatballs. So we can have the meatballs tomorrow instead."

Think how brief and sweet that conversation might have been with the help of extrasensory perception.

"What's for dinner?"

"Baked pork chops, of course."

"*Baked pork chops!* Splendid! Just what I wanted."

"Yes. I knew."

One of the late James Thurber's many worries was the possibility of a war between the sexes. He didn't mean the cold war, which has been going on since Eden, but a real shooting war, in which women generals would ride horseback and give orders, waving swords, and women enlisted men would fire howitzers at men enlisted men.

He needn't have worried. Women could no more organize a war than they can organize a cocktail party. They would surely be undone by their peculiar inability to communicate.

I was lying by the pool at Dalton's one Sunday, listening to the women trying to organize what they called, forgive me, a "girl lunch."

I think Ilya Ransome started it. She probably had another baked ham she couldn't get rid of.

"Why don't you all come over to my place," she said, "like Tuesday?"

"Tuesday what?" my wife said. I don't know why she had to get into it. Once you're in a thing like that it isn't easy to get out.

"Well, *Tuesday*," said Ilya. "Isn't this Sunday?"

"Yes," said Mrs. Dalton. "Of course it's Sunday. Just look at it."

"I know," my wife said, "it's Sunday. But I mean what Tuesday would it be? I mean, what's the date?"

"Let me see," said Ilya. "Friday was the thirteenth. I know because my husband said it's supposed to be unlucky. But he doesn't believe all that nonsense. Well I do. I'm a Virgo."

"If Friday was the thirteenth," my wife said, "that would make today the fifteenth, wouldn't it? Because yesterday would have been the fourteenth. So Tuesday will be the seventeenth, because tomorrow is the sixteenth."

"Well of course it's the seventeenth," said Ilya. "That's what I meant. What about noonish? Let's ask Alice Mangle. I'm dying to see her baby."

"Alice Mangle?" said Mrs. Dalton. "I thought she was divorced."

"Oh, yes," said Ilya. "Well, who am I thinking of that has the baby?"

"You're probably thinking of the Colburns," my wife said. "They have a new baby."

"Colburn?" said Ilya. "Do you mean what's her name?"

"No," said Mrs. Dalton, *"they're* divorced."

"We'll have little ham sandwiches and then march up the hill and swim at the Moonses," said Ilya.

"But our pool isn't heated yet," said Mrs. Moon.

A little cloud of despondence enveloped the group.

"Why don't we have a swim first *here?*" said Mrs. Dalton. "And then we could march down the hill and have little ham sandwiches at your place."

"What a perfectly marvelous idea," said Ilya Ransome. "Except I'm not sure I can make it Tuesday. It may be my day for yoga."

"I don't think I could make it either," my wife said. "It's the day of the PTA brunch, or is that Thursday?"

"Besides," said Mrs. Dalton, "I think the Mangles are still together. Isn't the little Mangle boy the one who broke his arm?"

"Well, why don't we make it Friday, then?" said Ilya.

"What date is that?" asked Mrs. Dalton.

Trying to work out the simple appointments of one's daily life is difficult enough. But communication in such abstract areas as art and history are near to impossible.

I remember a talk we had one night about the Mexican War. I think it was Curt who started it. He wanted to know what the United States and Mexico were fighting over, anyway.

"If you ask me," I said, "the whole thing was a mistake. But I wouldn't want to be quoted on that in Texas."

My wife was silent. I could tell she was trying to remember what the Mexican War was. Finally she put her knitting down and looked up.

"What *was* the Mexican War, exactly?" she asked.

I wasn't too sure myself, after so many years. We passed over it rather lightly in grammar school. But I believe the head of a house has an obligation to give an impression of limited omniscience. It steadies all hands.

"You never heard of the Mexican War?"

"I've heard of it, yes," she said. "But I've forgotten the details. Was that the one John Wayne was in?"

I sighed. "Is that the only way you can remember any history? The movies?"

"You know what I mean. *The Alamo*. That was it."

"No, that wasn't the Mexican War," I explained. "That was the Texas War of Independence."

"Well, there were Mexicans in it. I know that."

"Of course there were Mexicans in it. The Texans were fighting Mexico for their independence."

"Well, when was the Mexican War then?"

"I don't remember the exact dates. The dates aren't important. The important thing is why did we fight the war?"

"All right. Why did we?"

"We fought it to get California and Arizona away from the Mexicans," I explained, "and to get Texas into the Union."

"I remember now," she said. "Wasn't Walter Huston one of the heroes?"

"No, you've got that wrong, too. You mean *Sam* Houston."

"Of course. What's the matter with me? I always get Walter Huston and Sam Houston mixed up. It must be the similarity of names."

"Only Houston wasn't in it at all," I pointed out.

"Wasn't in what?" she asked. "You mean there *was* a movie of the Mexican War?"

"I don't mean any movie. I mean *Sam* Houston wasn't in the Mexican War at all. He was in the *Texas* war."

"Now I remember. You're right. He was in *The Alamo*."

"No, he wasn't in the Alamo. That's the whole point. He was somewhere *else,* trying to raise an army to *save* the Alamo."

"I meant," she said, "he was in the movie *The Alamo*."

We rested for a moment, gathering strength.

Then she said, "Now don't jump at me. Just say yes or no. Was Wallace Beery in it? I mean, did he ever play a role in it?"

"No. You're thinking of Pancho Villa. That was later."

"Oh, yes. That's right." She thought a moment. "Well, who was the big hero of the Mexican War?"

"Zachary Scott," I said. "He later became President."

She nodded. "I knew it was Zachary something."

The basic difficulty may be insurmountable. It may be that men and women were never intended to communicate, except in the most elementary manner.

Our anthropologists tell us that in the beginning the male was expected only to bring home the kill, and his mate to cook it, and there were no rhetorical exchanges beyond an occasional *ugh*.

For centuries the male regarded the female as a slave whose natural role was silent obedience. He is now being made to pay for those eons of domestic tranquillity. Woman is making up for lost time, and the more voluble she becomes the more dismayed her mate, conditioned as he is to blessed quietness.

Consequently the poor brute listens with polite discomfort to his helpmeet's monologues, fearful of making any response that might draw him into a dangerous dialogue.

Women shouldn't blame their husbands for this reluctance. They can't help it. They're only helpless conditioned animals. Besides, a woman can always pick up the phone and call another woman.

It is a demonstrable scientific fact that women's capacity for idle talk increases as the square of their number. Thus, two women can talk for four minutes without saying anything, three women nine minutes and so on.

I remember coming home one evening with the kill and trying to see if we could get by with nothing but a primitive conversation. My wife was making a dress.

"Hi," she said.

"Ugh," I said.

"Bad day?"

"Ugh."

She went on sewing. I put the kill in the icebox and lay down on the couch. The silence began to annoy me. You'd think they would at least show some interest in what kind of a day a man had.

"Anything exciting happen at home today?" I asked.

"Nope."

We observed another five minutes of silence.

"It seems to me," I said finally, "that you'd have something to say when a man comes home. After all, woman has broken her bonds. You're not a slave any more."

"I gathered, by your manner," she said, "that you didn't care about communicating."

"That's my privilege," I explained. "I can't help it. It's my conditioning. Thousands of years."

I explained the male's role in the history of the race—the master-slave relationship. She went on sewing. The phone rang. She got up and went into the kitchen to answer it.

"Oh, hi, Betty," she said.

They were at it exactly fourteen minutes and twenty-two seconds.

Despite these discouragements, I have never given up trying to improve communications in our house. I've even tried to improve myself as a listener. I read somewhere that listening is actually the key to better communications.

One is supposed to listen mainly for the major topic, and then for subtopics, and not pay any attention at all to the small talk in between. This small talk is just a sort of filler, put in to separate the major topics and subtopics.

It sounds reasonable, as a theory, but I found out it can be quite dangerous in actual practice. Those filler words are full of peril.

I tried it one evening when my wife was telling me about the throw rugs in the living room.

"The carpet's down to the threads in front of the sofa where we used to have the coffee table," she said. It's what she later said she said, anyway.

"We really ought to get a rug to put there," she went on. "We need one for the front door, too. And in the hall in front of the bathroom. Everybody is going in and out of the bathroom all day."

She paused, apparently waiting for me to speak. I was trying to figure out what the major topic was.

"You're not listening," she said.

"That's just it," I said. "I *am* listening. Go ahead."

"Well, what do you think?"

"Think about what?"

"What I said. About the rugs for the bare spots."

"What was your major topic?" I inquired.

"What are you talking about?"

"I want to know," I explained, "what was your major topic. You must have had a major topic, a subtopic and some filler."

"Well good grief. I only asked you what to do about the carpet where it's getting worn."

"The carpet?" I said. "What's the matter with the carpet? I thought you were complaining about the bathroom. Too many people coming and going or something. I can't help that, you know."

"Why can't you ever listen to anybody," she sighed.

"That's what I *am* doing," I explained. "I'm trying to listen selectively. I don't want to be concentrating on a lot of filler and miss a major topic, you see?"

"Leaving out the filler," I said, "your major topic was that too many people are using our bathroom and we need a new coffee table."

She nodded. "Right."

The next day when I got home there were three small rugs on the floor. They were bright orange, the color of Halloween.

"What's all this?" I said. "Orange rugs?"

"I told you last night," she explained. "I said I was going downtown and charge three new orange throw rugs."

"I didn't hear anything like that," I said.

"Of course not," she said. "It was in the filler."

YOU DON'T LIKE EYEBALLS?

One of the curses of white collar suburban man today is impedimenta.

I can't leave the house in the morning without my inventory.

Fountain pen, pencil, change, billfold, knife, keys, pills, homework, handkerchief, checkbook, charge-a-plates, fingernail clip and not one but two sets of eyeglasses.

When they are getting me ready to go through the front door and out into the world it is like getting a man ready for space. There is an air of tension and anxiety. Sometimes after I leave the pad, they have to destruct me.

One morning, for example, as soon as I had brushed my teeth and knotted my necktie the countdown began.

"Billfold?" said my wife.

I patted my left hip. There was an empty slap.

"What pants was I wearing yesterday?" I asked.

"You were wearing the houndstooth," she said. "Or was that the day before?"

It wasn't in the houndstooth. It had fallen into an old brown shoe I only wear when it rains.

"Glasses?" said my wife.

"Where was I reading last?" I asked.

"In the bathroom. You said it was the only place you could get away from TV. You were reading an article on Existentialism."

"Oh, yes, of course. But that's not the answer. Existentialism, I mean. It's too nihilistic."

They weren't in the bathroom. They were in the houndstooth coat.

"I must have been reading with my long-distance glasses," I said. "That means I must have driven home in my reading glasses. Now I know why everything seemed blurry."

I went through the pockets of the houndstooth suit, my leisure pants, my pajama tops and my old raincoat and got $1.62 in small change.

"Where's my pen and pencil?" I asked.

"What shirt were you wearing?"

"It was the gray one with the French cuffs. I remember because I forgot the cuff links. The cuffs kept flapping all day."

It was in the clothes hamper with the pen and pencil in it.

She handed me my briefcase. It was an old *Saturday Evening Post* I carried my homework in. I could always tell it by the cover.

"You have your knife?" she asked.

I patted my right pants pocket. It wasn't there. It had to be wherever my key was. My key was still in the car. My knife was dangling from it on a chain.

"Don't let me forget my cuff links today, for God's sake," I said.

"That's a button shirt," she said.

There wasn't any time for breakfast. I got in the car and drove off without any handkerchief.

Later she phoned me at work.

"You forgot your pills," she said.

"What was I taking them for?" I asked.

"Your sinuses. They're clogged up."

"Well, never mind," I said. "I won't breathe today."

"You forgot your reading glasses, too."

I looked down at the datebook on my desk top. It was all blurry.

"Great," I said. "Then I'll be able to see driving home."

But a man gets attached to these trinkets. I remember the trouble I went to, trying to find a black knit necktie, when my old one came undone after fourteen years.

I went first to my regular men's shop to pick one up.

"Black knit, sir?" said the salesman, a silvery gentleman. "Afraid not. It's the buyer, sir," he added, with undisguised bitterness. "Won't buy knits, for some reason."

He suggested a shop which might be more respectable. "Be sure to ask for Dacron," he admonished. "Wool stretches."

I left in melancholy. Even if I should find a black knit, I was supposed to make sure it was synthetic. Didn't they trust wool any more —that sturdy textile in which the English gentleman subdued the whirling dervish and his lady subdued the aspidistra?

I wandered into a department store, not expecting to find a black knit wool tie but hoping, in that vast bazaar, to discover some trinket that would lighten my frustration.

A big department store gives a man a sense of participating in an economy of abundance, especially if he has a revolving charge account.

"While we're here," my wife said, "why don't we look in the furniture department for a chair. For you to watch TV in."

It was true, I'd been getting a stiff neck watching TV. We bought a black plastic chair that not only rocks backward and forward but also swivels to right and left.

"Now you can rock like Whistler's Mother," my wife said.

"Yes," I agreed. "And what's more I can do it sideways."

"Oh, look," she cried as I was signing up for the chair. "There's carpeting."

She sounded surprised, as if it was one hell of a coincidence. I happened to remember that carpeting was in exactly the place it was in the last time she lured me up there.

It was true, our living-room carpet was threadbare. We signed up for fifty-odd yards of carpeting at something-ninety-nine a yard. I can never remember what the number was in front of the ninety-nine cents in store prices.

The carpeting we ordered is synthetic. "Outlasts wool," the salesman assured us.

On the way to the men's department I stumbled into the gourmet department.

"I'll just be a minute," I said, "I want to price artichoke hearts."

The artichoke hearts were too high. But I did pick up a bottle of Chanson Rouge 1959, a Moselle, a Rhine wine and an Italian chianti, on sale, plus two cans of Japanese snow peaches and a tin of clams.

While I was a-berrying in this happy dell, my wife had gone on to the men's department. She bought me a black knit tie. It was nylon.

When we got home I showed it to my older boy. He has an eye for smart men's attire.

"Neat," he said. "How much did it cost you?"

"As close as I can figure," I said, "about $740.99."

After that experience I hoped I was finished with the minor problems of haberdashery. I couldn't foresee the affair of the collar button.

It started when I bought the English shirt with the tab collar. Buying the shirt was an accident. I was waiting in the Ivy League department for one of my sons. The salesman had me under surveillance with eyes like pearl cuff links. I thought I ought to buy something to put him at ease.

It wasn't until I got home that I examined the collar. It didn't have a button. Where the button ordinarily is, there was only a buttonhole. Attached to each collar tab was a loop. I realized something was supposed to go through the two main buttonholes and also the loops, gathering everything together in a clinch.

"What have I got myself in for?" I wondered.

I tried to figure out what kind of device would solve the problem. Vaguely I remembered something of the sort.

"I could sew up the buttonhole and put a button on it," my wife suggested.

"No," I said. "I remember now. It's a collar button."

"Collar button?"

"Yes. My father used to have one," I said. "Remember, in those old movies, where the man was always down on his hands and knees in his underwear, looking for something?"

"Was that a collar button?"

"Certainly," I said. "Maybe you can pick me one up tomorrow at the dime store."

I could hardly wait to get home the next night. I hadn't been so excited since I sent away for the electric drill.

"Did you get it?" I asked. "The collar button?"

"They didn't have any," she said. "The girl didn't even know what one was."

"It's all right," I said. "I'll stop in a men's shop tomorrow at lunch."

I went to a place where I had once bought a pair of cat's-eye cuff links. They didn't have a collar button. The young man was baffled.

"I'm not sure I know what one is," he admitted.

I tried to explain—about the two buttonholes and the two loops. It isn't easy. I failed.

That night I looked up collar button in the Merriam-Webster's Unabridged. The next day, when I tried another shop, I was ready.

"A collar button?" the clerk asked.

"Yes," I said. "It's a button-sized stud consisting of a disk joined by a shank to a smaller disk, knob, or hinged flap, and used for buttoning a collar to a shirt."

His eyes widened. "Excuse me a moment," he said, "I'll get the manager."

I finally found a collar button in one of those elegant shops which appear to cater to Anglophiles who spend all their afternoons at the racetrack. They had two collar buttons, hidden away like jewels in a velvet drawer.

"Great!" I told the salesman. "I'll take them both."

"Sorry, sir," he said with a haughty smile. "I'm afraid we must limit ourselves. One to a customer."

I swore never to get down on my knees to hunt for the thing.

My worst experience with haberdashery, though, was one morning on a business trip to New York City. A man is supposed to be able to buy anything in New York, even if it's against the law. But I can tell you it's a hard place to buy cuff links before nine o'clock in the morning.

I woke up in the Americana Hotel one morning, fourteen stories above the streets of Gotham, and put on my last clean shirt. It had French cuffs. I picked through my suitcase in growing alarm. Yes, she had forgotten to pack my links.

I put on my coat and overcoat and found that, by hiking up my shirt sleeves, I could make the unfastened cuffs vanish, although it left my wrists cold.

I sneaked down to the hotel's jewelry shop, but it wasn't open yet. And a good thing too. There was a pair of diamond links on display in the window for eighty dollars. I consider diamonds too flashy for morning wear.

I walked down Broadway looking for a haberdashery. They were all closed. But everything else was open, including an upstairs dance palace that invited me to come up and dance with sixty beautiful girls. Who wants to dance at eight o'clock in the morning without any cuff links?

I decided to try a drugstore.

"Cuff links?" the druggist said. He looked at me as if there was something odd about buying cuff links at this time of day, even in New York. He puttered around his counters and finally came up with a pair.

"These are nice," he said. "Only a dollar-fifty."

They were made to resemble eyeballs.

"Don't you have anything else," I asked, "aside from eyeballs?"

"You don't like eyeballs?" he asked with an air of incredulity.

"It's not that I don't like eyeballs," I explained. "But I don't like eyeballs for cuff links."

He looked about some more and came up with another pair. They were replicas of the Empire State Building in brass.

"It's not only a cuff link," the druggist said. "It's a nice souvenir."

"They're beautiful," I admitted. "Like the eyeballs. But I don't think I care for the Empire State Building as a cuff link."

"Well, maybe I got the Chrysler Building," he said. "How would you like that?"

"Never mind," I said. "I'll just try to get by without cuff links."

He shook his head. "You're a hard man to please, mister," he said.

I felt foolish. A grown man in a great city, unable to buy a pair of cuff links. I thought of going back to the hotel and waiting for the jewelry shop to open. I could take the diamond links and charge it to the Diner's Club.

So I'd look a little flashy, I told myself. What's wrong with a little flash when you're in the Big Town?

I thought of sending my wife a telegram and asking her to mail me a pair. Special delivery. But I was afraid that might alarm her. Telegrams upset women.

I was getting quite hungry. But I didn't want to go into a restaurant with my cuffs flopping about.

I went back and got the eyeballs. I've grown to love them.

Cuff links and collar buttons are vexations, but buying a new suit is one of the most trying of male experiences.

No matter how handsome a new suit may have seemed in the store, it gives me a start when I take it out of the box at home.

For one thing I'm color-blind and can't see very well otherwise. Also the lights in men's stores are unlike any light a man is ever likely to stand under in life.

Once when I went to buy a new suit I made the mistake of taking my wife with me. Not to tell me what I liked but to tell me what color it was. I buy my own pants in this family.

I pawed about a bit on the rack and found a gray coat that seemed to fit. I studied myself in the three-way mirror. Gray flatters me.

"How do you like it?" I asked my wife.

"Are you sure you want a stripe?" she said.

"What stripe? It's a solid gray, isn't it?"

"Gray? It's brown."

"Brown? Are you color-blind? It's a dark gray. Kind of a charcoal."

"Maybe the *stripe* is kind of a gray. But the *suit* is definitely a brown."

"What stripe?" I turned to the salesman for help. He avoided my eyes.

"It's a perfect fit, sir," he said. "You are a perfect thirty-nine. Did anyone ever tell you that? You should be a model."

"Can I step out on the sidewalk," I asked him, "and take a look in the sunlight?"

"Go right ahead," he said. "I'll just hold your old coat."

In the sunshine, I admit, it seemed to have a stripe. I really couldn't say whether the coat was brown or gray. It was somewhat the color of a field mouse I saw once.

"I'll try on the pants," I told the salesman. Whenever I decide to try on the pants I am already dead and I know it. I haven't got the nerve to try on the pants and not buy the suit.

The salesman sensed this weakness. He summoned the tailor.

"Um hmn!" the tailor said. He circled me in admiration. "A perfect thirty-nine!" he said. "You should be a model."

"Aren't the sleeves a bit short?" I asked. You have to watch those tailors. They hate alterations.

"You wear cuff links?" he asked.

"Sometimes," I admitted. "I have a pair of eyeballs I bought in New York."

"You want your cuff links to show," he advised me. "The sleeves are perfect. You should be a model."

When the suit was delivered a few days later I lifted it lovingly from the box. It was a kind of olive green.

"Ye gods!" I cried. "They've sold me a chameleon."

"Don't get excited," my wife said. "I'd call it a gray. But I can't see any stripe. That's odd."

I still don't know what color it was or whether it had a stripe or not. It fit superbly, though. Maybe I should have been a model. But when I put the suit on I felt more like a field mouse.

One thing I always try to avoid is a sale. I panic in those mobs of aggressive women. But needing an electric toothbrush, I ventured into a department store to look them over one morning and got caught in a month-end sale.

I had no idea it was the end of the month until I got to the store and saw the phalanxes of women pressed against every door, waiting for the opening. I should have known then that something was amiss.

When the doors opened I surged in with one of the phalanxes. The women sprinted off in all directions, like a soccer team taking the field; lips compressed, eyes determined.

A burly gray lady who looked like a female chiropractor grabbed my coat sleeves.

"Young man," she said, "where are the handbags?"

"I don't know," I said, "I'm looking for toothbrushes."

She eyed me suspiciously. "Don't you work here?"

"No," I said. "Do you?"

She stomped off.

Somehow I found myself in the men's clothing department looking at a rack of sports coats marked down to thirteen-ninety-nine or fifteen-ninety-nine or something-ninety-nine.

A woman came up to me with a brown checkered sports coat on the hanger. She looked like a Vassar gym instructor.

"How much do you weigh?" she demanded.

"Hundred and sixty," I said. "How much do you weigh?"

She held out the checkered coat. "Would you mind trying this on? It's for my husband. I couldn't buy it without trying it on."

I took off my jacket and put the coat on. She stood back and eyed me.

"No," she said. "You're too thin. Wait here."

She hurried back to the rack. I took off the checkered coat and was slipping into my jacket when she came back. She handed me a coat I would have to call orange.

"Try this one," she ordered. "It's a thirty-eight-long."

I put on the orange coat. It was a bit too small in the shoulders.

"No," she said. "He's bigger than that."

When she went back to the rack with the orange coat I decided to make my getaway. I drifted over to a table piled with marked-down slacks. By happy chance I found a pair of yellow ones my size. I'm fond of yellow.

I went to a dressing room and put the yellow slacks on and went out in the tailor shop to look at myself in the mirror. The lady gym instructor pounded up.

"There you are!" she chortled accusingly. "Say—you planning to take those pants? They look like my husband."

By God, I promised myself, *if she tries to take these pants off I'll fight.*

"Here," she said, "try this on." She handed me a red plaid jacket with large bronze buttons. I put it on over my yellow slacks.

"What do you think?" she asked.

I looked at myself in the mirror. "Frankly, madam," I said, "I wouldn't wear this outfit to a dogfight."

"Well," she said, "you don't have to be snippy about it." She marched off.

I never did find the electric toothbrushes. I bought the red coat instead.

WOULDN'T YOU SAY WE'RE WEALTHY?

I have tried to teach my sons the value of money, and how to handle it. A sounder foundation in money management wouldn't have marred my own youth any.

I still have some records in my desk of my elementary fiscal dealings with the boys. I even encouraged them, as unskilled laborers, to form a union. They called it the C & D Smith Union. I can laugh now.

It seems ironical that an organization which so often was antagonistic to my own welfare should have borne my name. Of course it was their name, too.

I knew I had labor-management trouble the first time Douglas handed me a bill. It was headed *Smith Union,* in a baroque scrawl, and it listed the following items:

2 mixes of morter for wall	$1.00
1 lawn mow, upper and lower . . .	$1.50
1 week feeding cat	$1.00
2 weeks allowance	$2.00
Totle	$5.50
Plus lone	$1.50
Totle	$7.00

My first reaction was to despair of the lad's ever learning to spell. Then I was struck by the full implications of the document. It was larceny.

"What are you trying to pull?" I demanded.

"It's my bill, Pa," he said.

I remembered telling them it would be wise to keep books. Document everything.

"All right," I began, "what's this about feeding the cat? Whose cat is it?"

"Ours."

"Right. Then you can feed him on your own time. The cat is your own responsibility."

"Okay," he said. "Skip the cat."

"What do you mean," I went on, "'Plus lone'?"

"The loan you borrowed," he said, "to get a haircut. It was a Saturday. You said your cash was all tied up."

"I don't remember borrowing any dollar fifty from you to get a haircut," I said.

"You didn't get the haircut, Pa," he said. "You got some beer instead."

"Oh, yes," I said, with a deprecating laugh. "I remember now. The barbershops were closed. It was a holiday, I believe."

"Yes," he said. "It was Mother's Day."

I scanned the bill again. There had to be some error.

"How about this two mixes of mortar, one dollar? You are only supposed to get a dollar an hour for hard labor and you know you can mix two mixes of mortar in half an hour."

"That was a separate deal, Pa," he explained. "We mixed the mortar for Ma that Sunday morning when you were in bed. You said it would be worth double to let you sleep."

"All right," I conceded. "A deal is a deal. But this whole thing is extortion. You give me a bill for five dollars and you still want two dollars allowance. For what?"

"Pa, sometimes we don't get any work to do, like when your cash is tied up. You said we ought to have an allowance. You said it was for security."

"Hmm," I said. "That must have been the day I bought the beer."

Anyway, I had won the issue over the cat. But I still felt I was holding the short end of the contract.

"You men don't even realize," I said, "about fringe benefits."

"What's that?"

"That's all the things you get for nothing. Who pays for your clothes and your food and gives you a place to sleep and pays the dentist because you don't brush your teeth?"

"You do, Pa, but you get fringe benefits, too. Like we make our own beds and pick up after us and all that stuff."

"All right," I said. "I'll pay this one. But we've got to renegotiate. And you work on your spelling. You hear?"

I noticed that his older brother was in deep concentration over some papers.

"Get on with your homework," I told Doug. "Like your brother."

"This isn't homework, Pa," said Curt. "I'm figuring up your bill."

Despite these early hardships I believe my policy of instilling a sense of fiscal responsibility in my offspring was not only admirable in concept, but, in the long run, efficacious.

I felt pride the first time one of them was able to lend me a substantial amount of cash in a temporary period of insolvency.

He extracted five dollars from a book called *Sam Houston: Savior of Texas*.

"That's a poor place to keep money," I told him, folding the fiver and slipping it in my billfold.

"Well," he said, "I knew where it was, and nobody else did."

"Where did you get five dollars, anyway?" I asked.

He said he got one dollar for washing the car, one dollar for digging the hole, one dollar gambling, thirty-five cents for the sale of a lizard, a dollar fifty allowance and the rest he saved.

"Gambling!" I exclaimed. "Who've you been gambling with?"

I don't like them gambling. It teaches the wrong values.

"With you," he said. "Remember the Pirate-Dodger game?"

"Oh, that," I said. What a disaster that had been. The Dodgers had the game on ice in the bottom of the ninth and Drysdale threw Clemente a gopher ball a debutante could have hit over the scoreboard with her parasol.

"What hole are you talking about digging?" I asked.

He said I paid him a dollar for digging the hole under his horizontal bar.

"Why should I pay you for digging your own hole in the ground?" I asked. "I must have been out of my mind."

"You said paying a man for a good job was a way to perserve the dignity of the common laborer," he said.

"The word is *pre*serve," I told him. They can dig holes, traffic in lizards, and gamble for a living, but still they mangle the English language.

I was alarmed by the entire situation. I investigated the other boy's financial accounts and discovered he had twenty-nine dollars saved up in a drawer with his socks and track ribbons.

"That's outrageous," I told him. "How did you ever manage to accumulate such a fortune?"

He said I had paid him twenty-one dollars for building the wall, at one dollar an hour; his grandmother had given him a two-dollar bill for Christmas; he had four dollars left from selling mistletoe and the rest was the result of canny dickering with other financiers of his own generation.

"Why should I pay a mere boy a dollar an hour for menial labor?" I grumbled. "I must have been out of my mind."

"You said it was the minimum wage, Pa," he said. "You said if I did a man's work I should get the minimum wage. You didn't want to get in trouble with the law."

"Well, that's bureaucracy for you," I sighed. "It's making paupers of us all. When I was your age I was lucky to get twenty-five cents an hour."

"Well," he said, "that's when there wasn't any minimum wage."

I thought of telling them it was also a time when there wasn't any money, but I doubted if they'd understand that. They believe there was a World War II, because they've seen the movies. But nobody makes any movies about the Depression. It wasn't romantic enough.

"Has it occurred to you," I asked, "that you ought to work for nothing, as a matter of filial obligation?"

"What's filial obligation?"

"It's like the Depression," I explained. "Nobody believes in it any more."

That wasn't quite fair. They offered to work for nothing. But if they were to be paid at all, they insisted, they should be paid the minimum wage.

"We wouldn't want you to get in trouble," Curt explained.

It may seem in casual review that I have been the loser in these contractual relationships. But in truth, more often than not I have profited.

There was the Saturday morning, for example, that I got the car washed for nothing, saving myself a dollar nineteen cents. That's what they charge at the wash rack.

That was the day I planned to take the boys and a couple of their friends to Pacific Ocean Park for an outing. Then I had this splendid idea.

"Why can't the boys wash the car?" I suggested to my wife.

"I don't know why not," she said. "Except for you. You're the one who says they aren't slaves. You say they're not supposed to do menial chores while they're in pursuit of higher education. The peaks of Parnassus, I think you called it."

"I know," I said. "That's true. Alexander the Great never had to wash his father's car. But if they're going to go somewhere in the car, they ought to wash it."

I woke the boys up and told them my idea.

"Why sure," said Curt. "Can we ask the other guys over to help?"

"Certainly," I agreed. I was pleased. I realized he was thinking along the same philosophical lines I was. Whoever was to benefit from the car should help wash it. The consumer must produce.

The other boys were on hand early that morning. They all set to. It was gratifying. They swarmed over the car with water and polish and inexhaustible energy.

It only took them two hours. There were distractions and interruptions, too. Young Victoria, who lives next door, came over and sat on the wall and regarded the entire performance with female cynicism. She is studying to be a *femme fatale*.

"Is it all right," Curt asked, "if we make some breakfast?"

"Of course, certainly," I said. "Workingmen have to eat."

My wife and I went down the hill to the market in the little car.

When we got back the big car was drying in the sun. It gleamed. The boys were playing baseball in the street.

"Nice work!" I shouted. "Looks great!"

When I got in the house I found my wife staring dumbly into the icebox.

"Good heavens!" she exclaimed.

"What's the matter? What's wrong?"

"We're out of *eggs!*" she said. "That isn't possible."

"How many eggs did we have?"

"A dozen," she said. "At least. And the bacon."

"The bacon. What's the matter with the bacon?"

"It's gone too. A pound, at least."

I looked in the bread bin. There were two pieces of bread, if one counts the heel.

"Anyway, they didn't clean us out," I said.

I made a jelly sandwich.

"Look at it this way," I pointed out. "We got the car washed for nothing, didn't we? It could have cost us a dollar nineteen."

"Yes," she admitted. "I have to hand it to you."

She started washing the dishes.

Our sons have grown up in prosperous times. It is hard to convince them their father is not exactly a rich man. I had a chance to point out this truth one evening when Doug mentioned a schoolmate of his who had to run barefoot at track meets because he didn't have any track shoes.

"Why is that?" I asked.

"I think it's because he's poor," Doug said. "I mean his folks aren't rich."

I saw my opening. I had been waiting a long time for the felicitous moment to explain to my family that we weren't rich, either. They are the kind of innocent middle-class, American people who are always saying, "And it only cost a dollar ninety-eight," as if a dollar ninety-eight fell out of the air, like raindrops.

"I suppose you think *we're* rich," I said.

"No," he said, "I know we aren't rich, but we *are* wealthy, aren't we?"

"I would hardly say that," I told him. It seemed to me to be the moment to strike. "We have nothing more in this world than I bring home by the sweat of my brow."

It was a corny phrase, I admit, but the sooner they learn clichés the better.

"To be wealthy," I explained, "is to have enough money that you don't think about it. It's like getting a drink of water in the kitchen. You just turn it on until you've got as much as you need at the moment, and you never wonder where it comes from or whether it might run out."

"I still think we're wealthy," he said. He got up and went over to the new Merriam-Webster International Dictionary, for which I had paid $47.50. I thought it would encourage them to look things up.

"It says here," he read, " 'Wealth: Abundance of things that are objects of human desire; abundant supply; large accumulation.'

"Don't we have an abundance of things that are objects of human desire?" he asked.

I looked around. The living room was cluttered with objects of human desire. On the cocktail table alone there resided Volume Three of the World Book Encyclopedia, a can opener, a tennis shoe, a Boy Scout knife, an unexpurgated edition of *Lady Chatterley's Lover,* a pepper mill, a box of Kleenex, a letter from my bank, a paint brush, and a number two iron.

"Yes," I had to admit, "we do have an abundance of things that are objects of human desire."

"Then wouldn't you say we're wealthy?" he asked.

"Yes," I sighed. "We are."

I didn't have the heart to tell him that because I had forgotten the check I had written to Merriam-Webster for the dictionary, in which he looked up how wealthy we are, the letter on the cocktail table advised me that I was five cents overdrawn and that I owed them a two-dollar charge on a ten-dollar check they had bounced.

The boys have come a long way since they charged me a dollar for a hole in the ground. They may drive a hard bargain, but they do honest work.

One morning I went out to inspect a concrete walk they were building below the garage.

It was amazingly well designed, with a bold curve and an upward sweep like the ramp of the Guggenheim Museum in New York. But the second step disturbed me. It was ten inches thick. It must have taken fourteen sacks of readymix concrete.

"What did you think you were doing?" I asked. "Pouring piers for the Chrysler Building?"

Curt appeared unperturbed.

"You told me," he said, "to build things that would last."

"I know, I know," I said. "But do you realize that nobody will ever use this walk but little children and dogs and a woman pruning roses?"

"You told me," he said, "to build for the centuries."

"Ah, yes," I sighed. "I remember." I had been reading *Ancient Times,* by Dr. Breasted, and was profoundly moved by the instincts that had made those Egyptians build beyond their own horizons.

I stamped on the step. It was massive and magnificent. Solid as the Great Cheops itself.

"All right," I said. "Carry on. Mind you mortar up around the edges there. Otherwise you'll have beetles in the cracks in a thousand years or so."

We are building for the ages.

YOU'LL HAVE IT AS LONG AS YOU LIVE

The older a man gets the better acquainted he becomes with doctors, dentists, optometrists and their ilk.

Most of us don't have much contact with such practitioners until our molars, livers, or wives start giving us trouble.

Like a driver in the Indianapolis five hundred mile race, after so many laps around the track a man has to make a pit stop.

I finally went to Dr. Reap's office for a physical. If I were a Duesenberg Special instead of a human being I would have needed new tires, rings, points, and shock absorbers.

The doctor couldn't find anything much wrong with me that I hadn't already diagnosed. If they can't turn up something unusual they feel frustrated. It's my opinion that when they can't find anything wrong there shouldn't be any charge. That's the way it is at a gas station. There's no charge for air, water, and friendly reassurance.

"Wait a *minute,*" Dr. Reap said suddenly as I was buttoning up my shirt. "What do we have here?" He was examining my X ray. He seemed excited.

He had discovered, he explained, something quite extraordinary. "Look," he said, showing me the X ray. All I could see was a structure that looked like a Christmas tree.

Dr. Reap called in his associate, Dr. Withers, a cadaverous man who looked as if he hadn't laughed since the First World War. He looked at my X ray. His face lit up. Finally he said something in Latin and shook his head in wonderment.

"You don't see many like that," he whispered in a tone that reflected deep professional gratification. "Quite rare, indeed."

Dr. Reap and Dr. Withers patted each other on the back and smiled warmly, as if they had just delivered sextuplets.

"What *is* it?" I demanded when the associate left the room, chuckling.

"Your rib cage, Jack," said Dr. Reap. "It's festooned with calcium deposits. Like a—like a—*Christmas* tree."

"My God!" I groaned.

"Don't worry about it, old man," he said. "Perfectly harmless. You'll have it as long as you live."

"Thank God for that!" I sighed.

I have never known a dentist socially. But I got on intimate professional terms with one who pulled an old wisdom tooth of mine. Bottom left. I say it was old. I suppose it was a few years younger than I am. But I knew it well. I hated to part with it.

They said it had to come out because it wasn't any damn good and would turn on me someday. I tried changing dentists, never going back to the same one twice. But they caught up with me. They have a conspiracy.

When I surrendered at last the nurse took my name and got me to climb into one of those starkly efficient chairs.

"Roll up your left sleeve," she said. She was a pretty blonde.

"For what?" I demanded uneasily. I didn't want anybody to fool with my arm. My teeth are in my mouth.

"We're going to put you to sleep," she said. "With Pentothal. You won't feel a thing."

"Not me, you're not!" I cried. "Nothing doing. My heart isn't any too good this morning. I'd die right in this chair."

Her tender brown eyes regarded me with gentle scorn.

"Ninety percent of our patients prefer to be put to sleep," she said. "We just put you to bed after it's over."

"What's all this?" It was the doctor. Friendly, competent-looking chap. He was wearing some kind of a spyglass on his forehead. It made him look like a unicorn.

"This gentleman wants a local anesthetic, Doctor," the nurse said. "He doesn't want to be put to sleep."

"Wants a local, eh," said the doctor. He squinted at me. He looked at my tooth through his spyglass.

"Make it easy on yourself," he said. He rocked the chair back and said, "Open your mouth." The blonde moved in close and peered into my mouth with great, tender, brown eyes.

The needle found its mark. I stiffened like a scorched lizard and stared popeyed at the nurse. I tried to say something flippant. "Glaaa," I said. She didn't get the message.

The doctor went away. He came back and tapped my chin.

"Numb, is she?" he asked.

"Yah," I gargled. "Dub."

He nodded. He lifted a cloth on his instrument table. His eye expertly scanned the assortment of tools. He selected a combination can opener and shoemaker's awl.

It was over in no time. He tossed aside the tooth that had so long been part of me.

I realized the occasion called for some insouciant remark. I decided on, "Wasn't it H. G. Wells who said, 'We die piece by piece'?"

The blonde stuck a gauze plug in my mouth.

"Glaaa," I said.

While I was undergoing all this rehabilitation I also got myself measured for a new pair of eyeglasses.

I'd been keeping my last pair in my coat pocket. They didn't work. They also made me look like Steve Allen, which is all right for him but not for me.

The doctor said he would like to see them before we began the tests. I handed them over. He turned them this way and that, squinting at the lenses. "Aha!" he said.

I tried to explain why they weren't any good.

"I have astigmatism in my left eye," I said, "so that everything is blurry. When I don't wear any glasses my right eye sees whatever I'm looking at and my left eye wanders off like a cat.

"When I put on these old glasses I can see better out of my left eye. It stays on the subject and things are clear. I can also see better out of my right eye if I am looking at a distance.

"But if I am looking at something close up, I can see better out of my left eye, but still not as good as my right eye, but my right eye doesn't see as good as if I took the glasses off. And of course if I do that my left eye wanders."

"Yes, of course," said the eye doctor, "like a cat." He held my glasses up and squinted at them again. "Aha," he said, but without much zest.

He turned off the lights and had me look through an optical device at one of those charts with lines of block letters, each line smaller than the one above it.

The top line was V O E G C.

He covered my left eye and had me read it with my right eye. I was perfect.

"Excellent!" he said. "Excellent!"

Then he covered my right eye and had me read the line with my left eye. I got it again. He seemed surprised.

"Why, you shouldn't be able to read that, Mr. Smith," he said.

"I didn't," I said. "I remembered it from reading it with my right eye because it spells voegc."

He looked at the chart. "Why, so it does," he said. "I'd never thought of it."

Then he had me read the smallest line with my right eye. It was V P O U G M E C G H L E.

"Excellent," said the eye doctor. "Now, let's see you read that with your left eye."

The line looked like a black caterpillar.

"V P O U G M E C G H L E," I said.

The eye doctor studied the chart carefully. "Mr. Smith," he said, "does that spell something?"

"No," I said. "I had it memorized."

As it turned out, he had his own tricks. After that he made me read the lines backward. I can't memorize backward.

Then he made me look at a screen on which were projected a ball of light and a long thin line of light, like a billiard ball and cue.

He said for me to tell him where the ball and the line were in relation to each other.

"Above," I said.

"Good," said the eye doctor. "And now where is it?"

"Above," I said, "only more so."

"That can't be," he said.

"Well," I said, "that's where it is."

"What is?" he said.

"The ball," I said.

"Oh," he said. "I was talking about the line."

"Well," I said, "I was talking about the ball."

He said I had a problem and would have to wear bifocals. Nothing doing. They make me look like Harry Truman. That's all right for Harry but not for me.

Finally I had to go to Dr. Rue, my osteopath, to find out what the trouble was with all my left shirtsleeves. For the last few years I've noticed that the cuff of my left sleeve always stuck out from under my coat an inch more than the cuff of my right sleeve.

I told the doctor about it one morning when he was adjusting my sacroiliac. I had never gone to a doctor specifically about my left sleeve. Somehow I felt diffident about going to a doctor just to tell him that one sleeve was longer than the other. There are so many people in the world with worse problems. But this seemed like a good chance to bring it up casually.

"I want to show you something, Doc," I said. I slipped my coat on.

"You see that?" I said. "It's the same with every left sleeve I have. What d'you suppose causes it?"

The doctor folded his arms and looked thoughtfully at one cuff and then the other.

"You know what's causing that?" he said. "You're putting your left arm too far down in your sleeve."

From then until my next appointment I practiced not putting my left arm in so far, but the cuff always stuck out farther than the right one anyway. I reported this to the doctor.

"I was afraid of that," he said. "We'll have to have X rays."

At the X-ray laboratory, a formidable nurse led me to a dressing booth. She handed me a white kimono, the kind that opens down the back.

"Take off everything but your socks and put this on," she said. "Open side in back."

I have never been able to tie a bow behind my back, which is one of the reasons I'm so reluctant to have X rays. When I came out she tied my bows and stood me in front of the machine.

"Stand very still," she said. "Now take a deep . . . deep . . . breath. Now . . . let it out. Now stand very . . . very . . . still."

My eyes closed. I dreamed I was standing in front of a firing squad.

"You're falling!" the nurse shouted. I woke up. "Oh, my," she said. "We'll have to do it all over. You spoiled that one."

"I fell asleep," I explained. "You hypnotized me."

"This time," she said, "keep your eyes open."

When I went back to the doctor he already had the X rays.

"Look at that," he said gleefully, pointing to my left hipbone. "You see anything odd?"

I certainly did. My left hip was lower than my right.

"Five-eighths of an inch," the doctor said.

"Remarkable!" I exclaimed. "How do you account for it?"

"Simple," he said. "Your left leg is five-eighths of an inch shorter than your right leg."

He told me to wear a lift in my left heel, to make my left leg longer. This made me feel taller than before, especially on the left side.

But my left sleeve still stuck out too far.

Actually, my visits to the doctor's are rare. I'm sort of an amateur physician and physical therapist myself, and have generally managed to keep my body fit without the tinkering and tampering of professionals.

On my own, with no tools of research but a mirror, a thermometer and a wrist watch, I discovered the glich, the blurk, and the druzzles. These are subtle and elusive afflictions that even the cleverest doctor might overlook on a house call.

The symptoms are agonizing, if invisible. In the glich, the victim experiences headache, nausea, both low and high blood pressure, and an alternating tic. I have heard this called Sunday morning sickness, but that is a misnomer. I've had it on Saturdays, too. Bed rest and baking soda are indicated.

The blurk is similar to the glich except for an aching in the small bones of the ear lobes, myopia, rheumy eyeballs, and a general feeling of melancholy. Nothing can be done.

The druzzles is the worst, being a combination of the other two, aggravated by a hatred of society. Stay home from work, take the phone off the hook, lie in bed with the sheets over your eyes and curse the world.

The last time I had the druzzles I took my own advice. I could have gone to Reap, but he would only have scoffed at my diagnosis, given me an unctuous lecture and packed me off to work.

"It's all in your mind," he would say.

When I woke up I was breathing through only one nostril and the leg opposite the good nostril had a twitch from the kneecap to the ankle. I got up and staggered to the bathroom and looked at my tongue. It was the color of an old avocado peel.

"Call the office," I told my wife, "and tell them I am sick and won't be to work."

"What will I say is wrong with you?"

"How do I know what's wrong with me?" I snapped. "Am I a doctor? Tell them anything. Tell them I'm dying. Tell them one of my lungs isn't beating."

She called the office and told them I had a virus. I suppose that's what they expected to hear.

Later I was dozing in my sun-filled bedroom when she came in.

"I have to change the sheets," she said. "It's washday."

"Go ahead," I told her.

"With you in bed?"

"Why not? They do it in hospitals. I have prescribed complete bed rest for myself. I'd also like an alcohol rubdown."

I got up while she changed the sheets. You have to humor them. Besides, I wanted to see what was in the icebox and get a book. I had a glass of grapefruit juice and picked out a volume of Sherlock Holmes. By then the bed was made. It was luxurious. New sheets are soul-satisfying. Agreeing to get out of bed while she made it up had been worth the effort.

"Very neatly done," I told her. "You should be a nurse."

"What do you think I am?" she said.

"How about bringing me my cookbook," I said. "I want to look something up."

"*Your* cookbook?"

"Yes. Remember the one somebody sent me? *The Breakfast Cookbook*. It's all about breakfast."

She found it. I got up on one elbow and began looking through it for a good recipe.

"D'you think you should be up on your elbow like that?" she asked. "I thought complete bed rest meant flat on your back."

"You have to use your muscles," I explained, "or they get flabby." I changed to the other elbow. "Here's what I want. Tomato soup and egg."

"Tomato soup and egg? Whoever heard of that?"

"'Including an egg in your soup,'" I read, "'is not merely a good idea—it is brilliant.'"

"How do you make it?"

"'Simmer soup and milk three minutes and add egg. Poach egg until done and serve with toasted English muffin.'"

"I haven't got any English muffin."

"Think of something," I said. I sank back on the pillow to rest.

I opened the Holmes. I decided to read *The Sign of the Four*. It's one of Conan Doyle's best. In a moment I was back in the London of Sherlock Holmes. I heard the rattle of the hansom cabs bouncing over the cobbled streets in the yellow fog. I saw Holmes pacing his rooms at 221-B Baker Street, absorbed in the labyrinth of some exotic puzzle. Ah, those nostalgic tales!

She came in with my breakfast on a tray. "Will you prop up the pillow?" I asked. "I'm not supposed to sit up very long."

The soup and egg was superb, with just the right touch of Parmesan sprinkled on top.

After breakfast she stuffed the clothes and linens in the wash baskets and drove off to the Laundromat. I was left alone; perhaps, I realized, to die.

I dozed. The doorbell rang. I got up and went to the door in my pajamas. It was a zealous-looking youth with a bloodless face and silver-rimmed eyeglasses, carrying a large black Morocco book.

"Good morning, friend!" he shouted, pushing his scrubbed white face toward mine. He flipped his book open to a place marked with a purple velvet ribbon. "Are you ready for the Judgment?"

"Not this morning, I'm not," I said. I told him to go away unless he wanted to witness an unattended and intestate death.

I went back to bed and burrowed in. The phone rang. I let it ring. Then it occurred to me it must be the office. They needed me at work. Some emergency had occurred. I picked it up. There was a pause at the other end.

"Mr. Smith!" exclaimed a female voice. "Are you home?"

"No," I said. "This is a recording."

"Were you asleep?"

"No. I was reading the Communist Manifesto."

The phone went dead. I was mixing a glass of baking soda and water when the doorbell rang. It was a neighbor lady. She turned gray.

"Isn't Mrs. Smith here!" she squeaked, her voice going quite out of control.

"Yes," I said. "I have her locked in a closet."

She backed down the steps and hurried away.

The phone rang. I knew it must be the office this time. They didn't believe I was sick. They didn't need me. I was fired. I answered with a sense of doom. It was a small boy.

"Is Doug there?"

I told him no, Doug was at his ballet lesson. He didn't believe me.

"Is Joe Rodriguez there?"

"Who's Joe Rodriguez?"

"He's our shortstop."

"The only shortstop I know," I said, "is Joe Tinker. He's not here. I haven't seen him in quite a long time. Thirty, forty years."

"Our shortstop's name is Joe Rodriguez," the boy said. "Goodbye." He hung up.

I was too weak to go to bed. I sat by the phone, waiting. A little girl called next.

"Guess who this is," she said. She giggled, by way of a clue.

I tried to guess. "Babs Hutton?"

"Oh!" she squealed. *"You're* not Curtis." She hung up.

That was a nasty bout of druzzles, but I was over it and back to work the next day.

I've always realized that nervous tension underlies most of the physical ills of modern man. When I reach home after a day of friction and stress out in the abrasive world I'm tied up like a Greco-Roman wrestler. My hands are knotted into small bloodless rocks like petrified octopi.

My stomach is taut as a trampoline. My neck turns in noisy jerks, like a ratchet. My optic muscles are stretched like slingshot bands, ready to let go and shoot the eyeballs right out of my head.

These are the classic symptoms of the contemporary malady, metropolitis, for which the double four-to-one martini, taken three times daily before dinner, has become the most effective and popular specific.

Some time ago, however, I determined to withdraw from any dependence on this treacherous narcotic. At the outset I had encouraging success with my new regimen of mild exercise, hydraulic therapy, and soothing phonograph records.

One day I came home so tense I was just a massive tic. I got into my sweatsuit and went to the garage for my workout. I use an old set of barbells a neighbor gave the boys.

You don't have to *lift* the weights at all. I found that I got plenty of relaxation if I merely bent over, grasped the bar and just *tried* to lift the weights. This stretches the muscles of the back, arms, shoulders, legs, and behind the kneecaps. By not actually lifting, one avoids the danger of rupturing something or dropping a cast-iron disk on one's foot.

Fifteen minutes of this and I was unwound. I could feel the gentle swell of blood in my capillaries. I was ready for the tub. The water should be body temperature. Get in when the tub is empty and let the water gush over you, dancing and bubbling against the weary flesh.

I lay back in the tepid whirl. I squeezed my eyes shut and looked at the inside of my eyelids. Their fiery pictures soon faded. I pulled the plug. My tensions drained away with the water.

I dried with a rough towel. I put on flannel pajamas and lambskin slippers. I played a recording of languid Spanish guitar music. I sank in a deep chair and listened to the ripple and arabesque of vibrant strings. I was a golden leaf caught up in an autumn zephyr.

My wife's voice clanged through the mist like a train wreck.

"Didn't you *hear* me?" she shouted. "You got a notice this morning from the life insurance company. You've *lapsed* again."

"Any more mail?" I mumbled. My zephyr had died down. I was only an old dry leaf, falling to the cold sidewalk to be swept up.

"Only a card from Dr. Pragmire," she said. "He wants you to bring your cavity in before it's too late."

"What's for dinner?" I asked.

"I know you don't like it," she said, "but it was on special. It's liver and eggplant."

I got up and mixed a double martini.

Dear Lois:

I am embarrassed
that you had to buy
the books.

Without the tunes,
there wouldn't have
been any.

If you need
another set, let
me know. I'll be
more prompt.

Jack

TIDEPOOLS AND A CASTLE

In early summer Doug and I got away for a few days to camp on the shores of the Pacific.

Curt was tied up with algebra and modern literature in summer school. He also seemed to be tied up in some occult way with the telephone.

My wife stayed home to paint the living room a grayish beige and try to find out where the ants were coming from. They had been craftier than ever. I even found some in my desk. They were dismantling a Chinese fortune cookie I had dropped in the drawer. It said, *You have great self-discipline but you also have a breaking point*. How true.

We decided to go to the beach instead of the mountains because I have an affinity for the sea. I was born within a hundred yards of the surf. All my life I've felt its surging tides in my blood and heard its boom in my ears. Of course, that could be hypertension.

We drifted up the coast to San Simeon, that picturesque little cove below the late Mr. William Randolph Hearst's unlikely castle.

Gradually I became attuned to primitive harmonies and rhythms. It took me three days to quit listening for the telephone.

The first morning I was awakened by the fog. It managed to creep inside the tent and clog all eight of my sinuses. It also made my tennis shoes clammy and dampened breakfast. However, I fried our eggs without breaking a yolk and so started the day with a sense of mastery.

We walked a mile along the beach and sat on a rock, studying the primeval struggle for existence in the swirling pools left by the tide. Then we sat on a driftwood log in silence, waiting for the fog to lift, half-expecting that some eternal truth might be washed up at our feet in the foam. I felt momentarily profound.

Finally a wave surged up higher than the others and drenched our feet. So all that came to me from this timid supplication of the ocean's wisdom was wet shoes.

We squished along the beach over spongy carpets of seaweed and stones as smooth as plums, scattering seagulls. The mist hung over us like an organdy veil, then fell back from a blue sky.

The sea turned from gray to blue and seemed less forbidding. Doug put on his red trunks and rubber fins and mask and clamped his snorkel in place and paddled into the surf looking like some monstrous throwback in the long story of man's rise from the slime.

He floated harmlessly on the surface like a golden bug with a red abdomen and black prehensile snout, doubtless creating panic in the well-ordered underwater world.

A hundred yards down the beach I saw what appeared to be a black football bobbing in the waves. It turned out to be a seal that had upped periscope for a look around.

Seals may be friendly to amphibious humans—I don't know. But I believe in rendering to seals what is theirs. I waved Doug in and we hiked back to our camp for a lunch of liverwurst loaf and cheese nips.

Later, we overtook a little girl walking along the beach barefoot. As we drew near she turned around suddenly and let us have the full impact of her appearance. Quite incongruously, she was wearing a hideous orange and black Halloween mask. I recoiled in what I hoped was a satisfactory demonstration of horror.

She lifted her mask. Her eyes were wide and anxious.

"Did I scare you too much?" she asked.

"No," I assured her. "It was just about right."

I was unwinding after all. One day sooner and it would have scared me too much.

I found that between Sebastian's store and the inside of our tent, life in the outdoors wasn't unbearable.

Lying there in my sagging army cot, which ran ten degrees down-hill, wrapped in the chill arms of the fog, I felt as cozy as a larva. There was no need to stir until time to break out of the cocoon and find something to eat.

Through Sebastian's, the clapboard general store which had endured the moods of the Pacific shoreline since 1852, I was able to establish a tenuous but heartening lifeline back to civilization.

During his reign in the opulent castle on the sunny mountain above our cove, William Randolph Hearst maintained daily contact with the capitals of his empire by means of teletype machines inside the walls and telephones in the gardens. They were attached to convenient trees like owls.

Doug and I had no such elaborate communications system. However, we got off a collect call one night from the pay phone at Sebastian's to our home base and arranged for a money order to be mailed in care of the San Simeon post office in the rear of the store.

As we waited for this reinforcement we made a study of our fellow campers. Americans love to pack up and run away from the stable communities and comforts they have built. Every morning our small campsite was a-crawl with nomads. From the tent window it had the look of an army stirring awake from a night's bivouac.

There on the bleak shore they busied themselves demonstrating the American love of gadgetry. Station wagons as big as boxcars rolled up under the eucalyptus trees, in a few minutes disgorging an astonishing arsenal of ingenious hardware. And in a few hours it was all swallowed up again and the wagons pushed on to the next night's encampment.

These road people were an odd-looking breed, with their raw and windblown faces and their hair as tangled as seaweed. They were swaddled in clothing as ill-assorted as a rummage counter heap. They walked with a simian crouch, from sitting in cars most of their lives.

They were a hardy and self-sufficient folk, though, and seemed to practice a philosophy of live and let live. They spoke various tongues, mostly akin to English.

We were disgruntled when a rawboned and leathery old couple nosed their station wagon up near our tent and pitched their own, blocking part of our view of the foggy shore.

Our feeling of being rudely handled grew deeper when the aromas of some succulent stew began washing into our tent on the sea air from their campfire.

Later we went out and gave them a stony look. They were tidying up after their homecooked repast. The stew still simmered in a big pot. The man looked up.

"You boys had your supper yet?" he said.

We were caught off balance.

"Well, no," I said, "we were just fixing to start it."

He lifted the lid of the pot. A cloud of perfumed steam swirled up.

"More'n enough for me and Mama," he said. "You better have some. It's good."

We had to accept, of course, as a matter of courtesy.

It was excellent. I'd like to have the recipe, but I never got it. In an hour the old couple had pushed on.

Doug said it tasted to him like nothing more than potatoes, carrots, onion, and meat, salted and peppered and boiled over a campfire by good people.

Finally we succumbed to the lure of Mr. Hearst's castle and took some smug satisfaction in the discovery that his million dollar Roman bath was leaking.

Mr. Hearst's Casa Grande, the main structure of this astonishing pile of masonry, sculpture, and vainglory, gleamed against the sky like a freshly scrubbed mirage, its Moorish towers flashing in the sun.

It all looked most improbable. It might have been something one of Walt Disney's bright young men had painted on the sky. One expected it to fade out suddenly and be replaced by Donald Duck or Greta Garbo.

We parked at the base of the castle road and went up the hill in a yellow bus with the other tourists. On the way I counted three zebras. A lady sitting near the front on the opposite side claimed she saw either a mountain lion or a llama.

We were met at the castle steps by a young woman who said she was our guide. She warned us not to touch the statues. She said our fingers were oily. This was a wise precaution. The lady who thought she had seen a llama had been eating a hot dog on the bus and her fingers were not only oily but also mustardy.

Our guide really knew her castle. She was a fountain of lively facts and delivered her spiel with zest and wit. She also had as good a pair of legs on her as any guide I have ever seen in a museum.

I don't truly understand the fascination a real castle has for ordinary people who have never lived in one. Its effect is magical. In the great dining hall I could easily fancy myself sitting at Mr. Hearst's ancient table among that glittering company of thirty years ago, feasting on oriole tongues and drinking of Château Mouton-Rothschild '29 and effervescent gossip.

I wondered if Mr. Hearst's guests were permitted to toss their bones over their shoulders to the dogs, like Mr. Charles Laughton in *The Private Life of Henry VIII*.

"Dinner was served very formally," the guide was saying, "but oddly enough the condiments were brought to the table in their original containers. A jar of mayonnaise and a bottle of catsup often sat beside a solid silver chafing dish."

"See," I whispered to my son. "Your mother thinks I'm the only one."

In the guest house known as Casa del Monte I beheld with awe the bed of Richelieu. I half shut my eyes and fancied I could see the bony Cardinal within its ornate grasp, the covers drawn up to his gaunt nose, his eyes afire with sleepless cunning as he plotted some new duplicity.

"I must ask you not to touch the furniture," said the guide. I withdrew my oily fingers from the Cardinal's footboard.

We went on to the Roman bath. The gold and lapis lazuli mosaic ceiling was leaking. We weren't allowed inside, lest it collapse and bury us like so many Pompeiians. But we could peek through a window. I saw dimly the statue of a Roman nobleman.

"Look!" I whispered. "The young Scipio Africanus?"

Doug peeked in.

"It looks to me," he said, "like Bill Mazeroski."

After we saw the castle we drifted down the coastline from San Simeon to Pismo Beach in search of better surfing. San Simeon is an enchanting cove but the waves break directly on the beach. The dauntless body surfer no sooner surrenders himself to one of these monsters than he is hurled down to the sand. The sand is not sand at all, but millions of rocks the size of peaches. It is much like being struck in the chest by a rack of poolballs, a sensation one does not soon forget.

Besides, the water was cold. Only a man made of lard could enter this freezing stew of seaweed and shell fragments without dancing on his aching toes, clasping his arms about his goosefleshed ribs and uttering great, voiceless cries of anguish. This is humiliating to a man who used to float on his back at Waikiki, making up limericks in Pidgin English.

We were held up at San Simeon three days longer than we meant to stay because my name is Smith. This fact often gets me into a jam of one kind or another. I had told my wife on the phone to send the money order in care of General Delivery, San Simeon, California.

"You better use my full name—Jack Clifford Smith," I instructed her, "or it will undoubtedly be claimed by some other Jack Smith or J. Smith or John Smith or similar imposter."

We were three days finding the letter. Nobody could understand it. One gloomy morning the lady in the post office had an inspiration. There was, she remembered, a Clifford Smith stationed at the Coast Guard lighthouse at Piedros Blancos, a bleak outpost up the road a few miles. The lighthouse packet was searched, and there, of course, my letter lay.

It was a lesson to me. If your name is Jack Smith there is no use trying to get fancy with it. Your money will land up in a lighthouse.

Only a few years back, during the great depression, a penniless man could survive at Pismo Beach by digging clams. The broad beach, flat as a pool table, used to yield a daily living to any digger with patience and a back of steel, and an indestructible appetite for the clam's pearly flesh.

The clam has remarkably evolved through the millennia to serve gastronomical needs. He is a succulent animal, of a color women call beige, I believe, and almost wholly edible.

As they say of the hog, everything may be employed in one way or the other but the squeal. Clams, perhaps, do not squeal, but most likely, when opening and closing their shells, they creak. Especially as they grow older.

The Pismo clams are still plentiful, apparently, but their limitless availability has been diminished by the human population explosion. To express it biologically, people are multiplying faster than clams, despite the fact that the clam's sex life is subject to a good deal less tribal law. Our race is winning the battle for the tidelands, if nothing else.

The first night at Pismo we found out that my reflexes were still remarkably good in a penny arcade. It happened after dinner, which was splendid. We had pork chops over the fire. "Make sure they're not pink," my wife had advised us. They certainly weren't pink. They were what you might call black.

We boiled our tin dishes and tidied up the camp and drifted on into town. I can't stand to be away from some form of civilization for more than thirty-six hours.

Pismo may not be one of civilization's most elegant excrescences, but there are people there, a motion picture theater, a dance where lights of many colors spin around and around (but you have to be twenty-one to go in), some excellent restaurants, numerous bait and sundry shops, a roller skating rink and two penny arcades.

Penny arcade, of course, is just an old name. They are actually nickel and dime arcades. It's an example of inflation. When I was a boy, frequenting the arcades, you got ten shots at the Kaiser for a penny, and if you hit him eight times you got two extras.

The Kaiser is out-of-date. This generation never heard of him. But some things never change, like baseball. Doug and I played a nickel game of baseball in the penny arcade. A simple game. A steel ball rolls down a track toward a metal bat, which can be activated by the player. One watches the ball approach, and when it reaches the point where it is propitious to strike, one strikes. The ball then flies into a pocket marked "Home Run," "Double," "Triple," or whatever the case might be.

We played four games, forty cents, and I won eighteen runs to six.

A clear victory, beyond explanation by the rules of chance. Doug was quite upset.

"It can't be," he said. "There must be something wrong with the machine."

There wasn't anything wrong with the machine, of course. I knew it and he knew it. Somehow the old skill had come back to me. I was always good in the arcades, and it's something you don't lose easily.

We tried shooting at enemy aircraft. You pull the trigger as the image of the aircraft moves over the screen. It goes ta-ta-ta-ta-ta-ta-ta and every time you are on the beam a bell rings and a light goes on and you get one hundred points.

I won that one forty thousand to eight thousand. Why? Because, despite the ravages of time and luxury I still have the reflexes that made me the terror of the Class C basketball league.

After we bedded down for the night in our moldy sleeping bags, Doug asked me, "Pa, when you were a boy did you spend a lot of time around the penny arcades?"

It was the only explanation he could honorably accept.

It was a beautiful outing, but I was glad enough to get home. We had hoped to surprise my wife, but the car had developed a squeak. It gave us away.

We heard a cry. "Oh, no!"

Somehow it didn't have quite the note of rejoicing I had expected to hear. It was more a note of dismay.

We got out of the car and lugged our gear up to the front porch and opened the door, with a growing sense of foreboding. It was even worse than intuition had prepared me for.

My books stood in teetering piles on the living-room rug. The furniture was gone, except for the phonograph. It was playing *Never on Sunday*.

The French doors were swung wide open. The opening was occupied by the sofa, which was half in the house, half in the patio. The cocktail table was on the patio. My chair was on top of it. A dog was in my chair.

My wife was standing in the living room with my scarf around her head. She was wearing stretch pants and a sweatshirt. She was armed with the vacuum cleaner, a loathsome machine which I have asked never to be let into the living room in my presence.

It stood snarling between me and her, an ugly dragon with monstrous appendages and a tail that coiled around the room and plugged into the wall.

"I didn't expect you so *soon,*" she wailed. Her mood seemed conciliatory, apprehensive, and defiant.

"It's all right," I said. "I'll just get a nice cold beer."

"Oh, no," she said.

I went into the kitchen. The icebox was defrosting. The beer was warm.

"It's all right," I said. "I'll just take a nice warm shower."

"Oh, no," she said. "The water heater finally blew. I can't get the plumber. There isn't any hot water."

"It's all right," I said. "I'll just take a nap."

"Oh, no," she said.

I went into the bedroom. All the drawers from the chests were piled on the bed. They were covered by the curtains, which had been taken from the windows. The sun blazed nakedly into the room.

"I'm reorganizing," she said.

"It's all right," I said. "I'll just put on my trunks and lie in the patio."

"Which trunks?"

"You know. The white ones, with the red and blue stripes down the sides, like the Olympic Games."

"Oh, no," she said.

Anyway, she had painted the living room a warm beige. It was good to be home.

MAGRUDER

My friend Magruder is one of those wild and enigmatic people who enliven but complicate the lives of all who stray within their magnetic fields. Magruder is a meteorologist or something like that for the government, and he himself is very much like the weather—sometimes turbulent, sometimes balmy, and sometimes absolutely impossible.

He telephoned one night to offer me a fish. Instantly storm signals went up in my mind. Magruder is most treacherous when he comes bearing gifts.

"It's a sea bass, old man," he said. "A twenty-two pounder."

"I didn't know you were a fisherman," I bantered. I was stalling for time. I was pretty sure I didn't want a twenty-two-pound sea bass.

"I'm not," he admitted. "I just went along on this deep-sea trip to drink beer. Somebody else caught the sea bass. He gave it to me."

"Why didn't *he* want it?" I asked.

"He said it was too big for him," Magruder explained. "He's a bachelor."

"Well, why don't *you* want it?"

"I do want it. But I can't eat fish. I'm on this diet."

"I never heard of a diet where you can't eat fish," I said.

"It's a very unusual case," said Magruder. "I'll be right over."

He drove over with the fish. It was wrapped in a newspaper. He flopped it down on the sink and unwrapped it with showy admiration. The fish was two feet long. It was a dark gray. It had a light belly and great gray eyes with white irises.

"Ain't she a beaut!" said Magruder.

"To tell you the truth," I said, "I really don't think we need a sea bass right at this time."

"Are you crazy?" said Magruder. "You've got ten dollars' worth of fish here, man!"

"Well, I really don't think we can handle ten dollars' worth of fish," I said.

"Don't let it bother you, pal," said Magruder. "You can do something for me sometime."

He had a beer and left. I discovered that by rearranging everything in the icebox I could get the fish in. The last thing I saw as I closed the door was those woeful eyes, full of reproach.

"Don't blame *me*, old fellow," I said. "*I* didn't catch you."

When my wife came home I decided not to tell her about the fish right away. I didn't know what to say. Later she went into the kitchen and opened the icebox. I heard a shriek.

"What *is* it!" she cried.

"What's what?" I called out. I hurried into the kitchen. She and Magruder's sea bass were staring at each other in mutual astonishment.

"Oh, that," I said. "That's a sea bass. Magruder gave it to us."

"Well, I'm certainly not going to clean any big monster like that," she declared.

"Don't worry," I told her. "I'll give it to Dalton."

I phoned Dalton. "We've got this nice fish we'd like to give you," I told him.

"What kind of a fish is it?" Dalton asked. He sounded wary.

"It's a sea bass," I said. "A twenty-two pounder. It ought to make a hell of a *bouillabaise*."

"I don't think we can use it, Jack," said Dalton. "We've got this big halibut somebody gave us."

Our position was awkward. The fish was too big to put down the electric disposer. The garbage man wasn't due for three days. Eating it was out of the question, after having looked deep into those accusing eyes. I wrapped it back in the newspaper and took it down to the garage and put it in the deep freeze.

Magruder has mellowed since he became a father, somewhat late in life. He now affects the airs and gentility of a country squire. In his youth he was the holy terror of meteorology, or whatever it is he's in. Others quailed at the sight of him. He was, and is, the height and weight of a moose, with that formidable beast's great head and shoulders, spindly legs and aggressive mating instincts.

Magruder always gave colleagues the impression that he was in possession of information of the utmost secrecy and import. He raced in and out of rooms and up and down corridors with such speed that his coattails flew up behind him, like horizontal rudders. They called him Coattails.

Some years ago, in a moment of frailty, I lent my portable typewriter to Magruder to take to the South Pole. He was going down there as meteorologist with a scientific expedition.

I had misgivings. Magruder has a malignant influence on machines.

"What're you going to do with a typewriter down there at the South Pole, anyway?" I asked him.

"I don't believe I'm at liberty to say, old boy," he said. He always cloaks himself in great clouds of mystery. "But don't worry about a thing. I'll bring it back like Frank Buck."

The next I heard from him was by postcard from Auckland, New Zealand. *Wish you were here,* it said. *Shoving off for Antarctica tomorrow. Typewriter o.k.*

Then he vanished from human sight and knowledge, like Ronald Colman in *Lost Horizon.*

It was many weeks before I heard from Magruder again. He telephoned. He sounded far away.

"Where are you?" I shouted. I wasn't sure he hadn't called collect from Little America.

"Don't get excited," he said. "I'm home. I've got a bit of a cold. They don't heat their damn movies in New Zealand."

"How about my portable?" I asked. "Is it all right?"

"I was going to mention that," he said. "Funny thing. The *keys* are working too hard. It must have been affected some way by the cold. It was 30 below down there, you know."

I hurried over to his place. He was sitting in the kitchen drinking coffee royal and warming his feet in the stove.

"*Man,*" he said, "I'm not thawed *out* yet!"

He got the typewriter out. I tried it. He was right. The keys worked too hard. I took it home and let it sit a few days near the furnace. I thought it might thaw out. Nothing happened.

Dalton came over to take a look. He said it probably was the lubrication.

"She probably froze," he explained, "and it changed the chemical structure of the oil."

"What'll I do?" I asked him.

"Have her steamed out," he counseled.

Gribble came over. Gribble was with the Marines at Changjin Reservoir in Korea. He said the cold probably caused the graphite to crystallize.

"Happened to our machine guns at the reservoir," he said. "We had to thaw 'em out."

"How'd you do it?" I asked. "Out there away from nowhere."

He told me. It seems the Leathernecks thawed out their machine guns with the only warm water they had at hand.

"That's ingenious," I said in genuine admiration. "But isn't there some more conventional way?"

"Why don't you take her to a typewriter shop?" he suggested.

It seemed the sensible course. I drove it downtown and carried it to the shop closest to the office. It's a five-block walk, one-way. I told the typewriter man everything.

"We think," I said, "that it must have undergone some intrinsic change down there in the subzero weather. You ever hear of that?"

"Could be," he said. He tapped a few keys. "Works hard, all right."

He raised the cover from the ribbon shelf. There was a little lever by the right-hand spool. He put a thumb against the lever and moved it forward. He tapped a few keys.

"Try it now," he said.

It worked fine.

"Your tension lever was on too high," the typewriter man said.

Magruder phoned that night. "You find out what the trouble was?" he asked.

"The graphite was crystallized," I told him. Magruder will never accept a simple explanation for anything.

"Just as I thought, old man," he said. "What'd they do?"

"They steamed her out," I said.

Before the baby came, the Magruders lived in a flat with a noisy bathroom and a pull-down bed. Now they have a villa in the La Canada foothills, with built-in automation. When you open the bathroom door ultraviolet lights go on, beaming salubrious rays on the back of your neck. The kitchen looks like an electronic brain.

I remember the first time we went over to visit them after young Magruder was born. Magruder was sitting by the pool, sipping a gin and tonic and looking out over his acres to the blue mountains.

The baby was in the living room breathing conditioned air. He was wrestling himself in a playpen the size of a boxing ring. I would have liked to play in it myself.

"Don't you ever feel a little uneasy about all this?" I asked Magruder.

He looked thoughtful. "Only when the blasted thermostat's on the blink," he said. "Probably have to get a new one. Nuisance."

"Don't you ever worry about the rest of the world?" I asked. "India, for example?"

"Speaking of India," said Mrs. Magruder, "we're having a curry dish for dinner. It's yummy. It was the favorite recipe of some maharaja."

"Cooch-Behar," said Magruder. "The Maharajah of Cooch-Behar." He got up from his chaise longue and dipped a toe in the pool. "Curse this hot weather," he grumbled. "Makes the water too warm."

I felt myself struggling against lassitude. India floated far away. I splashed into the pool and climbed out refreshed and dripping, my sense of values restored.

"How do you fit all this into the economy, Magruder?" I asked.

"Economy? Don't know, exactly. We got most of it at Sears Roebuck. Have another gin and tonic."

"Didn't you ever hear of Pompeii?" I asked him.

He nodded. "Went there during the war. Bunch of ruins. Didn't build things to last in those days."

"Pompeii," I said, "is the symbol of the peril inherent in lust, greed, luxury, sensuality. It was destroyed."

My wife was lying on her back in the sun on a blue and yellow striped lounge pad, popping fat purple grapes into her painted mouth. A decadent Pompeiian matron.

"Umm," she purred. "This is the life."

"We are all corrupt," I sighed. I dived into the pool and swam strenuously, as if by physical effort I could escape the doom closing in upon us all.

We stayed for the curry. It was yummy.

We went to the Magruders on the boy's second birthday. He was asleep when we got there.

"He's getting a couple more teeth," Magruder told us. He tiptoed over to me like a mother bear and showed his teeth.

"It's these two," he said, pointing to his lower second bicuspids. Magruder's teeth, close up, are an awesome sight.

When the boy got up Magruder introduced us.

"This is Jack," he said in his Boris Karloff babytalk. "Say Jack."

The lad stared at me. "Auk!" he shrieked.

"That's right!" exclaimed Magruder. "Jack!"

Magruder explained that the boy was so attractive he was afraid to take him anywhere because everybody fawned over him.

"The women fuss over him so much it's embarrassing," he said. "Even the ones with kids of their own."

"Yes," I agreed. "That's bad. It could give him a Narcissus complex."

"I know." He shook his head glumly. "I've been keeping him home. But that's no good either."

"No. He's likely to draw within himself."

The boy had sneaked up on me. He snatched the pretzel from my hand. I started to snatch it back. He shoved a graham cracker at me. It was wet around the edges.

"Look at that!" Magruder chortled. "He wants you to have his graham cracker. Go ahead. Eat it. It's all right."

I nibbled at the damp graham cracker while young Magruder stared at me, crunching on my pretzel.

We went out to sit by the pool. Magruder brought out the baby photo album. I thumbed through it in the twilight.

"He's a beautiful child, all right," I admitted.

The boy came out and got on a fire engine and started racing around the patio, doing figure-eights, circling my chair and making a siren sound.

"*Hroom!*" He streaked in front of me on the fire engine, brushing my kneecaps. I flinched.

"Don't worry," Magruder said. "He drives that thing like he was born on it. Great eye for clearances."

"*Hrhoom!*" I held fast. He came from behind, whipped across my starboard bow, snatched the pretzel from my hand and ran over my right foot.

"Auk!" he shrieked, and was gone.

"You hear that!" shouted Magruder. "He called you Jack!"

Sometimes Magruder reverts. Deep down he still has the old appetite for adventure.

He phoned one morning not long ago and I sensed the old excitement in his voice.

"Come right over! Something fantastic has happened!"

"The last time you said that," I reminded him, "was when the kid rolled over all by himself."

"Forget that," he said. "This is really fantastic. I may need help. You have a gun?"

"Only an old single-shot twenty-two," I said, "without any bolt."

"Never mind. Come on over. We'll use my gun."

When we got there Magruder was sitting tensely beside the pool. There was a pair of binoculars in his lap. A cold wind raked the patio.

"It's cold enough for polar bear out here," I said.

"*Shh!*" said Magruder. "Come on!" He led us to the pool and pointed into it.

"What do you make of that?" he whispered.

I peered into the pool. It looked cold and murky.

"Needs a cleaning," I said.

"No, not that!" said Magruder. "The tracks, man! Look at the tracks!"

He got down on one knee and pointed across the pool to where the safety rope trailed down into the water. The inside of the pool was gray with a film of ash from a recent brush fire in the hills. A few clean splotches, resembling heel and toe marks, led from the coping into the depths of the pool.

Magruder told us his theory. Nobody in his household had been in the pool since the fire. The tracks must have been made by some intruder who climbed the fence and took an illicit swim.

"So what?" I said. "You going to shoot somebody for that?"

"You don't get it," said Magruder. "Notice anything unusual about those tracks?"

They did look odd. They were short-hauled, for human tracks, and there were only three toes.

"What do you suppose it was?" I asked.

"Maybe it was a sloth," said my wife. I realized I should have left her home. There was *man's* work afoot.

Magruder gave her a condescending smile. "No sloth around here for centuries," he said. He let us hang there a moment. Then he said, quite deliberately, "It was a bear."

"A *bear!*" I exclaimed. "How could a bear walk down the side of a swimming pool, for God's sake?"

"Simple, man," said Magruder. "He let himself down on the rope. See? The tracks face *upward*. He went down backward."

"Good Lord!" I cried. "But there aren't any tracks leading *out* of the pool. How did he get out?"

Magruder led us to the deep end of the pool. There were two marks like the others at the base of the ladder. "He let himself down by rope, swam under water to the deep end and got out by ladder," said Magruder.

I couldn't quite believe it. But there it was. "Where would a bear come from?" I asked. "There isn't a zoo within twenty miles."

Magruder scanned the surrounding hills through his binoculars.

"We think this is civilization," he said. "But they're out there somewhere, just over the hills, watching us, waiting for us to stumble and fall down."

"The other night," said Mrs. Magruder, "one of the neighbors said she saw a black panther. She called the sheriff. It was an opossum."

"They're cute," said my wife.

When we got back home I told the boys about the bear. They said bears have four toes. I phoned Magruder.

"Magruder," I said, "bears have four toes."

He seemed to think that over.

"Not *this* bear," he said.

The next time we went over to Magruder's I expressed some misgivings.

"What's the matter?" my wife said. "You afraid of the bear?"

"It's the boy," I explained. "I'm afraid Magruder's spoiling that kid."

"You're a grown man," she said. "You can take care of yourself."

It was right after a storm, and the street in front of Magruder's place was aswirl with mud washed down from the bluffs. Out in the street a Spanish-American War veteran was working with a shovel. He wore what appeared to be a Rough Rider hat, blue blouse, shirt and pantaloons, and black rubber boots. He had Teddy Roosevelt's ruddy face, clenching a cigar stub in his teeth.

"Whoever is that?" my wife said. "Somebody they've hired?"

"It's Magruder," I said.

"How can you tell?"

"It's one of his disguises."

We parked the car and got out and shouted at him. He leaned on the shovel and pushed his hat back and took out a great red kerchief and wiped his pink brow. The whole theatrical bit.

"Well, crease my britches!" he exclaimed. He affects period expressions such as that when he's playing a role.

We all tramped inside and Mrs. Magruder put on coffee.

"You want a belt of something?" Magruder asked. I told him just the coffee.

Young Magruder padded in like a Sioux. He transfixed me with suspicious eyes. He didn't seem to remember me.

"I'm the man," I reminded him, "whose feet you kept running over that day on the patio. With your fire engine."

This didn't reach him, but it served to type me in his catalogue. He left the room and came back with what appeared to be the cockpit of a B-52, or some such machine. His father got down on his hands and knees in the cockpit. He pushed a lever and a TV-like screen lit up on the instrument panel. A panorama of the earth, thousands of feet below, began rolling by. It created an amazingly realistic illusion of flight.

"Watch this," Magruder said. He pushed a button and a rocket was ejected from the machine. It zipped across the room and plinked into a glass door.

"You aimed at *glass,* Daddy!" screamed young Magruder. "You broke the rules!"

Magruder stood up sheepishly. He looked more than ever like a moose. "I forgot," he mumbled.

"Good Lord!" I exclaimed. "What an exhibition!"

"Fantastic, isn't it?" said Magruder. "It's all battery powered. You want to try it? It's just like actually flying."

"I better not," I said. "I get airsick."

Mrs. Magruder brought the coffee. "I think I'll have a belt of something after all," I told her.

"How did you like that?" I asked my wife on the way home. "That bit with the B-52."

"I thought it was cute," she said.

"Cute! A grown man down on his hands and knees playing with a toy?"

"It reminded me," she said, "of you and the boys when we got the war game. You took the Duke of Ellington's side, or whatever his name was, and lost the Battle of Waterloo."

"Wellington," I said. "It was the Duke of Wellington."

WILTED ASTERS AND NO SESAME

One morning in early August, I think it was, I accidentally slipped out of gear while doing nothing and managed to run idle for a few seconds. It is almost humanly impossible to do nothing at all, but once or twice in a lifetime it happens to a man.

Few of us have the insight to recognize and exploit these transcendent moments.

But there I was, suddenly, a lost thing out there somewhere in the void, beyond the pull of gravity or anything else earthly; beyond even the Nielsen ratings and the Gallup Poll.

I was sitting in my chair in the living room. With a part of my mind I was aware of that. I could see the yellow irises in the blue vase. But the television and the tables and walls had lost their magnetism and dimensions. They had no relativity to me. I was free.

I knew that somehow I had broken through the material wall into the infinite and that the answer to everything would spin into view and I could reach out and haul it in like a fly ball.

I was out there like this, waiting for the pitch, when my wife noticed me.

"Are you feeling sick?" she asked.

It brought me back. I reached out, too late, as centuries of wisdom hurtled by like a small golden sparrow headed for the outer stars.

"No, no," I mumbled. "I'm fine."

"I'll make you some tea," she said.

That's the way it is. Pure reverie is suspect. If a man gets his drive shaft disengaged from his flywheel they think he is having a stroke and make him lie down until the doctor comes.

Women especially don't trust anything that isn't tied down. They won't be much use in space except to tidy up around the rocket and set out antimacassars. They will keep scheming and nagging to go home. They will never have that weightless feel. Women have gravity built in.

There are exceptions, of course. I knew a girl named Lucille in grade school who used to brag she could make her mind a complete blank. She could, too; but she is one of the few women I ever met who had this useful faculty.

I never knew her to be tired or cross and she could run the fifty-yard dash in 7.5 seconds, wearing a middy and bloomers. That was quite good considering that tracks and coaching were primitive in those days.

Lucille married a good provider who manufactures radio tubes. She never let on about being able to turn herself off. A husband doesn't like his wife to have any unusual talents, especially one for which she was much pursued before he met her.

Most wives know this and are careful not to get caught in a state of disassociation. That is why even when they have switched off everything but their maintenance batteries they tend to keep doing some homely little thing such as knitting, dying their eyebrows, or watching TV.

But I often see men trying to disconnect themselves from the standard wave lengths and tune in on something way out.

I believe I can say that only twice in my life have I ever had a moment to do any real thinking, and both times it turned out poorly.

The first time was in the summer of '35. I climbed up on top of a boxcar on a siding in the desert one night and lay there looking up at the Milky Way and thinking.

Nothing ever came of it.

The second time was one summer weekend, when my wife took the boys out of town to visit her relatives. I knew my chance had come. I hurried home after work, impatient to get on with it.

The house was bare and still. I turned on one low light and lay down on the couch. Conditions were perfect. I felt like an abbot. I tried to concentrate on a bowl of wilted asters.

I wrote out a few basic subjects on scratch paper. *Life, what is meaning of? Disarmament, how? Human race, destiny of? Do I really need a new car? Is war necessary? What model?*

The phone rang. It was Mrs. Dalton.

"You poor thing," she said. "You're all alone. You better come over here and have dinner with us."

"I can't," I told her. "I'm doing some heavy thinking."

She hung up.

I couldn't blame Mrs. Dalton. She meant well. But I envied, for a moment, those monks and philosophers of earlier ages, who might spend many a serene hour uninterrupted by temporal affairs, considering some isolated question of magnificent inconsequentiality, such as why there are exactly so many petals on a flower.

I started in on *Life, what is meaning of?* This subject, I soon discovered, sounds deceptively simple. It is actually rather elusive.

I remembered I had to feed the dogs. I opened two cans of dog food and went outdoors to find the brutes. The phone rang. I set the dog food on the patio and ran in to answer it.

It was Magruder.

"Come on over," he said. "I've got this Old Crow."

People won't let a man alone. I told him about my project.

"Well, okay," he said skeptically. "Let me know if you run into any trouble."

I tried to remember where I had left off thinking. There was a scratching at the door. It was the neighbor dog. He grinned up at me. He had eaten the dog food.

I decided to move on to *Disarmament. Life, meaning of,* seemed too thorny at the moment. Anyway, I reasoned, if something wasn't done soon about disarmament, *Life, meaning of* would be a moot question.

I was thinking about the meaning of moot when the phone rang. It was my wife on long distance.

"There's some leftover lamb in the icebox," she said. "In aluminum foil. How are you? Is everything all right?"

I told her everything was fine except that I couldn't find the cursed dogs.

"We took them to the vet's this morning," she said. "Don't you remember?"

After we hung up I sat down in my chair and took my shoes off. The sun was already over the hill. I wondered what it would be like always to live in an unpeopled place, at this time of day, watching points and surfaces of light that one never sees when company, with all its urgent distractions, is there.

I realized that modern man is almost never alone, except maybe when he's in jail, and even then only when he has conducted himself with such hostility as to be thought deserving of solitary confinement.

Suddenly it was quite dark. "I'll light a candle," I thought, "and try to think of something serene." Better yet, it occurred to me, why not play some mood music on the hi-fi.

I turned on the light. I tried to find *Music for Medieval Reflections in the 20th Century,* but we didn't have it. I put on one of our old Spike Jones records, *Dinner Music for People Who Aren't Very Hungry.*

It cheered me up considerably. I went into the kitchen and unwrapped the leftover lamb. It looked insipid. I put it in a pan and smothered it with curry. I made a green salad and smothered it with garlic salt and celery seed. I made a piece of toast and was going to smother it with sesame seed. I couldn't find the sesame.

I phoned my wife long distance.

"What's the matter?" she said. She sounded concerned.

"Where's the sesame?" I asked.

"The sesame?" she said. "Hmm. I think we're out of sesame."

What kind of a woman would leave a man alone in a house with a bowl full of wilted asters and no sesame?

I decided to think about materialism. Have we become too dependent on gadgetry, forgetting how to live simply, using the resources within us?

The phone rang. It was Dalton.

"You all right?" he asked, keeping his voice low. He sounded conspiratorial.

"Certainly I'm all right," I said. These intrusions were beginning to crush my delicate mood. "Why shouldn't I be?"

He lowered his voice. "My wife says you told her you were doing some heavy drinking. She said you sounded half gassed already."

"Good Lord!" I exclaimed. "Heavy *thinking!* Not *drinking.* I haven't had a drop. Anyway, I have to hang up. My lamb is sizzling."

After dinner I went over to Magruder's to talk about life and help him out with his Old Crow.

EVERYBODY CAN'T BE A BALBOA

Late in the summer we spent a week at Ensenada, that poor and dusty Baja California town whose saving graces are the beauty of its climate and setting and the charm of its people.

It was the others who wanted to go. The botanists, linguists and primitives in the family won out. I wanted to stay home and read travel books. I don't know why we had to select for a family vacation a barren peninsula of which the author and adventurer Leonard Wibberley has written:

> There are some places in the world so remote that their very desolation and loneliness repel a man, and he quickly dismisses the thought of them from his mind, almost with a shudder.

"Oh, you know authors," my wife said. "Always romancing. Besides, you know very well we'll never get half a day's ride away from Ensenada."

"Half a day's ride on what?" I said. "A camel? Besides, you're wrong, as women usually are in these matters. What I'm afraid of is that once down there, at the end of the civilized world as we know it, I may succumb, as many other men have, to the mystic pull of the unknown, and plunge on.

"There's something inside a man," I continued, "that seems to be drawn, as if by a magnet, to the valley over the next hill."

"The last time we were in Ensenada," she said, "you seemed to have something inside you that kept drawing us to Hussong's Bar."

"It was the *mariachi* music," I explained.

Daydreaming among my books and travel guides, I began to see our proposed adventure in a new light. I could picture myself in the evenings, after the day's trek, my face burned by the unrelenting heat of the subtropical sun, my limbs heavy with the not unpleasant fatigue that comes of an honest struggle against the elements, taking that first sip of an icy *margarita* and shutting my hot eyes as Hussong's *mariachi* burst into that exuberant chant, *Ay! En El Rancho Grande!*

"Don't forget," I told my wife, "to pack my new Madras shirt and shorts, with the stripes."

We took a motel cabin in the heart of Ensenada as a base of operations, and the next day we packed a picnic lunch and set out for El Estero, a tidal estuary that invests the peninsula not far south of the town.

The estuary is filled by the surge of seawater spilling through a narrow opening from the Pacific. From its mouth, it strikes south beyond the eye's reach, ending somewhere under the shadowy hulk of Punta Banda, a rock like a small Gibraltar. At the mouth there is a resort consisting of trailer park, cabins, restaurant, and even a few luxurious apartments. But beyond this community there is nothing, until, at the south tip of the estuary, one comes upon La Grulla Gun Club.

One may rent a rowboat at the resort and row across the estuary to the sand bar which closes it off from the open sea. This bleached, unspoiled finger of land is my personal Shangri-La.

I had made several crossings to the sand bar in previous years, one or two of them hazardous. There was the time Dalton's son dropped the six-pack of Carta Blanca beer over the side and we had to skin-dive for it in a full fathom of water.

The Daltons weren't with us this year. I would have preferred his steady hand at the tiller, but we decided to cross on our own. The once hardy little fleet of orange rowboats was down to two. They looked forlorn. They tugged sadly at their mooring lines, like old dogs. I wondered what had become of their companions. We chose boat No. 1. She had the least water in her bilge and her paint was brighter.

"This area becomes dangerous from two to six o'clock, *señor*," the man in the resort office warned, circling the mouth of the estuary on his map with a red pencil. "Then the tide will be going out. *No?*"

I wasn't worried. I knew my years of boyhood training on the waters of Westlake Park would stand me in good stead. And, in fact, using my oar as a rudder and counting out the stroke for the others, I managed to get us across without mishap.

"Captain Bligh himself couldn't have done better," my wife admitted with open admiration.

We beached our craft on the sand bar and made our little camp. It was idyllic. For the moment the world belonged to us. Except for the occasional snarl of a speedboat or a distant sail, neither sight nor sound of civilization intruded on our isolation. The estuary shimmered under the hot blue sky.

I dug into our stores and lunched on a salami sandwich and a nectarine, washing them down with a bottle of chilled Carta Blanca. My wife was dozing under a Mexican sombrero. The boys were prowling the shallows with fins and snorkels.

Suddenly I noticed a dark dot far out on the estuary. It grew larger. I saw it had oars, which rose and fell awkwardly. The man was no oarsman, but he *was* making way. I realized the boat was orange. It was old No. 2.

"*Damn,*" I muttered.

In twenty minutes our visitors had beached. There were three of them—the man, a woman, and a boy. They settled a hundred yards to our north and opened a picnic lunch.

"*Damn,*" I repeated.

After a while, I strolled up the beach to get a closer look at our unwanted neighbors. As I drew near, I sensed I had seen them all before. I studied the little group covertly. Yes, definitely! Of course. It was the Gribbles, with young Harvey, from across the street. I had never dreamed Gribble was so intrepid. I walked toward him with outstretched hand.

"Old man Gribble, I presume," I said heartily.

"*Damn,*" said Gribble.

The next day, I decided we would strike deeper into the wilderness. The estuary was too crowded. We drove south until we came to San Vicente, a village founded by the Dominican padres in 1780.

Here we stopped at the town gas pump to fill up. The tank took eleven *pesos'* worth of ethyl. Ethyl, I found out, is a word that transcends national languages. When I told the gas man to fill her up he shook his head and smiled sadly.

"No English," he said.

"Ethyl?" I said hopefully.

Understanding lit his saddle-brown face. *"Si,"* he said. He patted a pump affectionately, like a used-car salesman patting a fender. *"Ethyl!"*

We left the paved road near Santo Tomas to search for the adobe ruins of the Santo Tomás de Aquino Mission founded by Padre Loriente in 1791. We never did find the ruins, but we met an ancient farmer who seemed to know where they were. We considered that a partial success.

We had been bouncing and yawing over the rutted road and were glad enough to pull up and let the car pant a moment while we talked with the old man.

He came down to the road from an adobe hut that was cooling itself in the shade of an oak tree. He looked exactly as such patriarchs should look, with skin like a dried chamois, a stubble of gray beard with whiskers as sparse as the cornstalks of his nearby field, and eyes that seemed to have seen some merriment in life. The absence of his two lower front teeth added a touch of drollery.

"Ah, *la missión,*" he said, nodding. I had got through again with a single word.

He shoved his sombrero back off his forehead and scanned the surrounding hills. Then he began pouring out a torrent of directions in Spanish, simultaneously pointing off in all directions.

"Gracias . . . gracias!" I cried at last, realizing I would learn nothing.

He bowed. He peered into the back seat and grinned at the boys. "No speak Spanish?"

"Hablo poco," said Curt. He talked with the old man. They seemed to reach some understanding related to the word *sandia.*

"He wants to give us a watermelon, Pa," said Curt.

"Si," I said.

We got out of the car and climbed to the adobe and stood on a patio shaded by branches while the old man went in the hut and got the watermelon. A woman's brown face appeared in a glassless window.

I offered to pay for the watermelon, although I sensed I was acting like a *Yanqui*. The old man raised his hands in protest and made a speech.

"He says he likes us and is content, Pa," said Curt.

That night when we got back to the motel the boys found a stray kitten, a calico about the size of a ball of yarn. They put it in a paper sack and began plotting at once with their mother to smuggle it back across the border. I would not, of course, allow it.

The next day I wanted to strike farther down the peninsula to the land of the *ocotillo* and that queerest of all New World plants, the boojum tree. But the others wanted to spend a day shopping.

It amazes me that people who live in the most productive country in the world can find so many things in Mexico which, apparently, they absolutely need.

I was determined to buy nothing but those articles necessary to sustain life, and which might be consumed on the spot, such as the local wine, the local tamales, and the local newspapers.

I wouldn't even go on their shopping expedition with them.

"Just drop me off at Hussong's," I said.

I waited out their vulgar spree in the cool of that old wooden-floored frame cantina which has been a watering place for American adventurers since the 1890s.

I was content to sip a *margarita* and listen to the *mariachi*. As luck had it, I did do some prudent trading while I was relaxing there, but I happen to know how to deal with the Ensenadans.

A small boy shined my tennis shoes for two *pesos*. A woman came in with a bucket on her head. It was full of hot tamales. I bought two for three *pesos*.

The boy who had shined my tennis shoes came back and sold me five packages of Chiclets for five cents, a shrewd bargain if I ever made one.

I gave the *mariachi* a dollar to play *La Bomba,* and a man came in selling tickets on the Mexican lottery. While I was dickering with him, the lady with the steaming bucket on her head came back with more tamales and the shoeshine boy came in with the *Ensenada Opinion,* followed by a man selling pearl-handled pocket knives. They formed a line.

I was thinking of ordering another *margarita* when my wife walked in. She was wearing a fantastic orange hat with a fringy brim. *Mexico* was embroidered on the crown in purple silk.

"Good Lord!" I exclaimed. "Where did you get that hat?"

"I got it at Maya de Mexico," she said, "for only two fifty."

A woman like that shouldn't be allowed to run around loose in a foreign country.

The next morning we set out to find Ejido Erendira, a tiny and isolated fishing village far south of Ensenada. I had never been there, but we were armed with a guidebook that told every turn of the way.

The guidebook was explicit. It said that at 46.1 miles south of Ensenada there was "a branch road right to a junction at 0.5 miles," and added that "the left branch is the best road to the coast . . . and reaches the sea at Ejido Erendira."

As I read it now, that passage seems clear enough. However, my wife was navigating at the time, while I drove, and she somehow missed the entire significance of the phrase "the left branch is the best."

We took the right branch, which is, I know now, not the best road, either to the sea or to anywhere else.

Having taken our fatal turn, we bumped along over dusty ruts through miles of wheatfields, up hill and down, slithering through muddy creek beds, skirting sheer one thousand foot precipices, raking our bottom over rocks and acquiring a growing feeling that we had perhaps left civilization too far behind and would never get back.

Eventually the road came to an end, for no good reason that we could see. We were all quite depressed, but I knew a little food and drink would help all hands.

We drove back to a glade where there were oak trees and a pond swarming with minnows. I called a halt for lunch. We broke out our supply of avocado sandwiches, beer and 7-Up and repasted in the wilderness. It was enormously quiet.

"I'm going to find the Pacific," I said, "if it's the last thing we ever do."

We rumbled back over the trail to a fork I had remembered. I got out and smelled the air. There was seaweed in it.

"On to Ejido Erendira," I said, and we set out. The hills seemed to be dancing about us. We conquered one only to have it reappear ahead of us. We crawled on for miles, raising no sign of life but lizards, squirrels, and now and then an owl. I kept scanning the sky for a seagull, but none appeared.

Finally a feather of dust arose in the distance. I stopped the car and listened. We heard the sound of an internal combustion engine. It was like receiving a message from the moon. We waited. In time a tractor came down the road. It was driven by a boy with a dusty face dark under a yellow sombrero. He stopped the tractor. We looked at each other in mutual astonishment.

"Talk to him," I instructed the boys, "and find out where the Pacific Ocean is."

They talked to him, with much waving of the arms, doffing of sombreros, *si señors* and *graciases*.

"He says," one of the boys reported, "that this road goes to the ocean, but it is twenty kilometers away."

It seemed too far. The sun was down behind the hills and I had no heart for creeping on this landscape in the dark.

"We'd better turn back," I said. "Everybody can't be a Balboa."

I wonder what might have happened if we had only taken the branch to the left.

There is an epilogue to our Mexican vacation. It concerns the calico cat. We did get the beggar across the border.

When the boys found the thing it was only two or three weeks old and locked in a mortal struggle with Mexican fleas the size of Egyptian grasshoppers. Everyone but me fell in love with this foundling and wanted to take it back to the United States. I explained that this was a sentimental and impossible fancy. Customs would never allow the cat across the border, and even if they did I wanted no part of a flea-bitten Mexican cat.

Ironically, the cat seemed to like me best, sensing, I suppose, that ultimately his or her fate was in my hands. I would wake up in the middle of the night to find it asleep on my neck. When it needed to answer nature's call, it always selected my swimming trunks.

I did help it get rid of the fleas. Maybe I don't like cats, but neither do I care to see them suffer. I rubbed it with vodka. Vodka is cheap in Mexico. The fleas rolled over and died like bulls in the Tijuana bull ring.

Whatever my personal feelings, I'm not one to go against the crowd. So when it was clear that all were for taking the cat home, I gave in. But I insisted everything had to be legal. There was to be no thought of smuggling.

I called the Tourist Bureau.

"*Ah, si,*" the man said. "It is permissible to take the cat across the border, *señor,* but he must be vaccinated."

We looked up a veterinarian in the Ensenada phone book and drove the cat to his office. Fortunately the veterinarian spoke English, *un poco.*

"*Ah, si,*" he said. "*El gato* is too little to vaccinate."

He directed us to El Edificio Municipale, where, he said, we might obtain a paper by which we could get the cat across the border. We drove to El Edificio Municipale. My younger son went in with me, carrying the cat. We worked our way through a number of beautiful Mexican office girls who obviously had no idea what we wanted but sensed that it was of the utmost urgency. We arrived finally in the august presence of the Chief Registrar. I explained our problem. He nodded.

"He was born in Mexico?" he asked.

"*Si,*" I said.

"What is his name?"

I remembered what the veterinarian had called him.

"His name," I said, "is *El Gato.*"

The Chief Registrar looked from me to Doug and back to me. His black eyebrows crept upward.

"*El Gato?*" he said uncertainly.

"*Si, señor,*" I said. "We call him *El Gato.*"

His excellency frowned. Then he saw the cat. A rush of pink suffused his brown face. He seemed to choke. Then he uttered a great asthmatic wheeze and began to slap himself on his plump thighs, rocking back and forth in his creaking swivel chair.

"Oh ho *ho!*" he cried weakly at last, fetching a vast handkerchief from a pocket and wiping his eyeglasses. "*El Gato!*"

"*Si, señor,*" I said. "*El Gato.*"

"I think," said the Chief Registrar, fighting off small attacks of hysteria, "I think all the time, *señor,* you mean *el muchacho.* I think you want to smuggle the *boy* across the border. *Comprende?*"

"*Comprendo,*" I said.

As it turned out, we didn't need any papers at all to smuggle the cat across the border.

WHAT'S GOING ON IN THERE?

Every man dreams of something he wants above all else. I don't mean abstractions, like liberty or togetherness, or the world's balkline billiards championship. I mean something frankly material, like a Mercedes-Benz, a gold-plated slide rule or a good used banjo.

What I want most in life is an extra bathroom. We already have an excellent little bathroom, but it's not equal to the traffic. I believe there are other bathrooms in the neighborhood, but apparently they are limited to adults only. Ours does a lively business in small children, many of whom I have never seen before.

They walk into the house unannounced, march straight for the bathroom and vanish, with a slam, behind its abused door. These sorties, I suppose, arise from playtime emergencies. They are distracting, but not the real problem.

The daily crisis occurs, as it must in most one-bathroom homes, during that peak traffic hour of rush and disorder in which all hands are preparing for their daily adventures in the outside world.

One morning it began as usual with the ringing of that infernal machine, the alarm clock. When the alarm sounds, Curt makes the first strike for the bathroom. He is young and agile and his room is closest. This gives him a split-second advantage that is usually decisive. We have learned to concede him the first round.

That morning the problem was aggravated by the failure of the lock on the bathroom door. It wouldn't lock. Some mornings it won't *unlock*.

Curt made his move as swift and sure-footed as a road-runner, slamming the door behind him even before I had the cursed alarm clock throttled.

Often I am second. Douglas tends to fall off to sleep after missing his first bid, and I make it to the door with a hop and a skip when I hear it opened.

This time I was outwitted. My wife had got up and gone into the kitchen and turned on the water, as if to make coffee. But then she stole back to the bathroom door.

When Curt emerged she darted in and whipped the door shut just as I sprinted up. It was like a quarterback sneak.

As it turned out I was dead last. Doug woke up just as my turn came and pleaded that his case was undeferrable. What can you do?

After he had been in the bathroom long enough I demanded, "What's going on in there, anyway?"

"I'm watching the birds," he answered.

There is a pomegranate tree just outside the windows. It is often full of birds, and a pleasure to watch.

I got inside at last and lathered my face. This is the most hazardous moment. I pressed the razor to my foamy cheek and the door flew open. It struck me in my shaving arm.

"Oops!" cried Doug. "Sorry, Pa! I have to wash my hands. I'll be late to school."

It wasn't really a bad cut, just a small stream of blood in the lather, like a red river in the snow.

It fascinated Doug.

"You cut yourself, Pa," he said, washing his hands.

Curt walked in.

"Why can't you knock?" said Doug.

"I have to brush my teeth," said Curt. "I'll be late to school."

I sat on the bathtub and held my head in my hands. When they left I finished shaving and got in the shower. For a moment I was gloriously alone. Curt came in.

"I have to wash my hands," he said.

"Don't kid me," I said. "You already did."

"That was Doug, Pa," he said. "You're mixed up. I brushed my teeth."

On the way out he collided with Doug.

"I have to brush my teeth," Doug said.

"I know," I said. "I know."

"Can you people give me one second," my wife said. "To comb my hair?"

Not being able to get *out* of the bathroom is almost as bad as not being able to get *in*.

This happened one day when I had arranged to meet my wife downtown at seven o'clock in the evening—an appointment with little chance of being kept promptly under the best of circumstances. I telephoned her at six o'clock to see if there was any likelihood she could make it by eight.

"I'll be there," she said, "if I can get the door open."

"What door?" I asked. I couldn't imagine what door she would have to open to meet me downtown.

"The bathroom door," she said. "It won't unlock again."

"All right," I said, "just keep calm. Follow my instructions."

I reminded her of the emergency key we keep hidden over the molding in the hallway.

"I already tried that," she said. "It doesn't work."

"Is there anybody *in* the bathroom?" I asked.

"Doug," she said. "He claims he's brushed his teeth ahead for the whole week."

"Tell him to climb out the window," I said.

"He claims it's undignified."

"Dignity sometimes must be suspended," I counseled.

Doug climbed out the window.

"Now," I told her, "you'll have to take the door off. Get a screwdriver and pull out the hinge pins and . . ."

"We've already done that," she said. "We still can't get the door off. It's stuck."

"All right," I said, "you'll have to climb through the window."

"What about *my* dignity?"

"See you at seven," I said, and hung up.

I'd like to have seen her climbing through the window in her robe, but I couldn't get away from the office.

She met me at seven-fifteen.

We finally had the bathroom tiled, on a Saturday. The tile men came in a pickup truck. They unrolled long strips of carpeting from the front porch through the living room and hall and into the bathroom. They took off the bathroom door.

They took the fixtures off the wall over the tub, ripped off the old wainscoting and mixed some plaster in a bin on the sidewalk. The neighbors began to gather. Anybody who doesn't do-it-himself in our neighborhood is regarded as an eccentric or a celebrity.

"It's all right to watch," I told everybody, "but please keep out of the way of the tile men."

The men went about their work with the calm, plodding certainty of artisans. It was beautiful to watch. The bathroom is only five by six feet however, and in no time at all there was standing room only, except for the Gribble boy. He was sitting in the washbowl.

"Mr. Smith," the head tile man said, "are all these children and dogs yours?"

"I don't know," I said. "Some days it's hard to tell."

We all had a cup of coffee and worked out a plan. My own personal children were allowed to stand at the bathroom door and look in. Any children I didn't claim were to take up posts along the route of march from the truck to the bathroom, provided they kept off the tile men's carpet. The dogs had to stay on the sidewalk.

When you are dealing with dogs, however, there is always one bad apple. One of my own brutes sneaked into the bathroom and got plaster on his nose.

We had ham and cheese sandwiches and beer for lunch. The head tile man ate slowly. He looked vexed and thoughtful.

"Mr. Smith," he said, "I believe I'd be willing to knock ten percent off the bill if you can get rid of all these kids and dogs."

The neighbor children grew quiet. Especially young Gribble. When children are quiet their eyes grow large and soft.

"I can't do it," I told the tile man. "We'll have to muddle through at the agreed price."

He was a man about it. Now we have a bathroom fit for a Roman emperor, although my wife says she wishes the color of the tile was just a little bit more on the eggshell side.

Even Gribble came over to give it a try.

"It's beautiful," he admitted, "but you've got a drip."

We've always got a drip.

Drips are the curse of modern plumbing. They drive you crazy. A drip at two o'clock in the morning can wake me out of a sound nightmare. A tub drip is insufferable.

A regular, reliable drip might be bearable. You could adjust to it. But they never are.

If you listen for a drip, it stops. If you quit listening, it starts up again. *Drip*. If you get out of bed to go find a drip it hides. You can sit in the bathroom and watch for a drip ten minutes and nothing happens but your feet get cold. The minute you crawl back in bed—*drip*.

It's too elementary a problem to call a plumber for. He would clunk around for two hours and charge twenty dollars and probably not fix the drip anyway. We fix our own drips.

Some time back, I admit, a drip I tried to fix in the bathroom was too big for me. I tried to get the handle off the porcelain water tank but the threads were corroded. I got a big wrench and put my shoulder to it. The tank cracked. The water ran out on the floor.

When the floor is an inch deep in water, it's time to call the plumber. When the plumber came he tried to get the cracked water tank off the bowl. He wheezed and grunted. Then I heard the now-familiar sound of porcelain cracking. It is not unlike the cracking of a ripe watermelon.

"Well," said the plumber with an unpleasant laugh. "You've *really* got trouble now, Mr. Smith. We cracked the bowl."

This job cost sixty-five dollars, parts and labor.

Later on we fixed a drip in the kitchen, without, I'm proud to say, any professional help. It was a week old and gaining strength. One keeps thinking a drip will go away, but it never does.

I sent the boys to the garage for my plumbing tools. Two monkey wrenches, a pair of pliers, a cold chisel, a hammer, and a tire iron. They couldn't find the Phillips screwdriver. We got in the car and drove down the hill to the hardware store and bought one for forty-five cents.

Using only the Phillips screwdriver, one monkey wrench, the cold chisel and the hammer, I got the handles off the sink faucet. The threads were quite stubborn.

We found out what the trouble was. The washers were worn out. We went down to the store for new washers. They cost ten cents. "You see?" I told the boys. "We'll fix this for only fifty-five cents."

We put the washers in and screwed the handles back on. The hot water wouldn't turn off. We took the hot-water handle off and discovered the trouble. Some idiot had mangled the threads.

We were going to the store for a new faucet but my wife said that as long as we had to get a new faucet anyway, why not get one of those with a hose and brush, that help you wash the dishes.

"You promised me one when we were married," she said.

We found one marked down to $42.95. But the old faucet wouldn't come off the wall. The threads were frozen. I phoned Magruder.

"What is it this time?" he said. "The toilet again?"

"No no," I said. "That's over and done with. It's only the kitchen."

"Boy oh boy," Magruder said, with a laugh that reminded me of the plumber. "That bathroom deal. What was it? Seventy, seventy-five bucks?"

"Sixty-five," I said. Magruder loves to exaggerate.

He came over, with a cigar in his mouth and an air of vast importance. He clamped an enormous wrench on the locked nut and leaned into it. He turned purple and bit his cigar in two. The nut turned. Magruder may not be very bright, but he can be useful in situations calling for brute strength. When he left we easily managed to do the more intellectual task of installing the new faucet.

When there's any really heavy plumbing to do, however, I generally let my wife handle it. That woman could really have been one of the great plumbers, except for the professional prejudice against her sex. I'm happy to say that I have no such feeling.

One weekend something clogged up the pipes under the house and water backed up in the kitchen sink. The disposer wouldn't work.

When the disposer doesn't work it's like in the old days when the chickens stopped laying or the cows got the grump or whatever they get.

You are stricken. Word gets around the neighborhood. People drop by to give advice.

Gribble came over and studied the sink. It was full of dark, angry water with bits of orange peel and eggshell like broken boats.

He shook his head like a quack doctor. "Smith," he said, "you got something backed up in your trap."

"I know," I said. "We're going to call a plumber."

It was a lie. We had no intention of calling a plumber. My wife had fixed these things before. She could do it again. But our ruse got rid of him.

We went to work. My wife got out the monkey wrench. I followed her outside. To get under our house takes vitality and know-how.

The crawl hole is on the uphill side of the house, so you can't crawl at it straight-on. You have to crawl down through a concrete retaining pit no larger than an old grocery carton.

First you get on your knees and elbows, lunge forward and drop into the pit on your elbows. The monkey wrench is held in the right hand. Now your knees are still on the ground above the pit. Then you put your head through the hole and crawl forward on your elbows seal-like.

One at a time you lower your knees into the pit. Your shoulders meanwhile hunch through the hole. You now have head and shoulders under the house, your elbows and knees in the pit and your feet on the ground.

If each step has been properly executed so far, nothing shows to the casual passerby but your posterior and the soles of your feet. Here is the critical moment on which success or failure hinges.

The left elbow and then the left knee are moved forward. The elbow goes under the house. The left foot is dragged over the edge into the pit. The posterior careens sharp to port. Quickly now, precisely the same movement is made with the right elbow and knee, the posterior first rolling to starboard, then leveling off and sinking into the pit.

The difficulty here is that the crawl hole will admit only a very low, or battlefield, crawl. So the torso has to be well advanced under the house and the posterior well lowered before the final thrust may be essayed.

It must be bold, sudden, and decisive. You grip the wrench, squeeze the eyes shut, and take two long strides forward on the elbows. As the body straightens, the legs shoot out over the top of the pit. The posterior dips low.

For an exciting moment the body is in the lovely classic crescent of the swan dive, except for the arms and the monkey wrench.

At this point you have risked all. You have made it or you haven't. My wife made it. It was one of her best, except for banging her head against a timber in the dark.

I went back in the house then. There was a lot of clinking and clunking going on under the floor. I could hardly read. When the noise stopped I went outside to watch her come out.

It was even more engrossing—like a woman in toreador pants crawling backward upstairs with a monkey wrench in one hand and her head in a barrel.

MAMA'S LADY IS OUT ON THE LAWN!

They say our homes in the 1980s—if any—will have luminous ceilings for controlled light. We'll be able to turn the ceiling on, like TV, and adjust it to suit the activity we have in mind—romance, badinage, or the pursuit of academic knowledge.

By the 1980s, I must expect, my pursuits will be purely academic. Even badinage may be too strenuous. But I'm ready now for luminous ceilings, considering the trouble I've had with floor lamps.

One in particular was a strange and evil instrument, and in some ways human. I first encountered it one night in my room. It was leaning over my desk, peering down at my typewriter with one of its heads.

It began at floor level like any normal floor lamp, with a round brass base for stability. From this the usual cylindrical shaft arose, carrying, I supposed at the time, its wiring. I believe now that it actually concealed some kind of primitive nervous system.

Where ordinary floor lamps blossom into decorative shades, this one degenerated into a pair of long and flexible necks, each ending in a bell-shaped head fitted with a searchlight. This bifurcated freak was unlovely enough in the daytime. At night it was hideous.

Our relations were amiable for a time. When I saw it standing there that first night I realized it must be some kind of gift from my wife. She loves surprises. I gave its switch a friendly turn.

A beam of white-hot light leaped out and bored into the typewriter. It ricocheted off the paper in the roller and crashed back into my eyes. My eyes are relatively weak.

I found the switch and gave it a turn. The light went out; but its mate went on. It stabbed me full in the face. I fell back, throwing up a hand to shield my outraged eyeballs.

I stumbled forward and seized the gleaming head by its neck. I gave it a wrench. The beam scraped crazily over the wall. The other head whipped around on its elongated neck and clapped me in the ear.

I gave the switch a turn. The head that had struck me glared on. Now they were *both* fired up. I gave the switch a turn. At last merciful darkness enveloped me. I groped to the wall switch and snapped it on. Soft light filled the room. In the light the floor lamp looked innocent.

I called my wife.

"Where did you get this—*thing?*" I demanded.

"Why, I got it with green stamps," she said. "Isn't that nice?"

"It's sick," I said. "It's schizophrenic. It has two personalities."

"Don't you like it?" she said. "It cost me four books."

"I loathe it," I said. "Take it out and kill it."

"It's only a floor lamp," she protested. "How can anybody hate an inanimate object?"

"Inanimate!" I scoffed. "Look at my ear." I showed her where the lamp had hit me.

"You've hurt yourself!" she gasped.

"*I've* hurt myself!" I sneered. "It was the goddam *lamp*. It tried to blind me."

"You're crazy," she said. She unplugged the lamp and carried it out. The next night it attacked me in the living room. One of the boys had come along and given the switch a turn. The beam caught me a glancing blow across the left cheek.

"Turn it off!" I cried, recoiling.

He gave the switch another turn. The light went out but its mate went on. It drilled me between the eyes.

"Again!" I shouted. "Turn it *again!*" I covered my eyes with a pillow. He gave the switch a turn. The first beam went on. It smacked me with a right cross.

Finally he gave it the fourth turn, or *coup de grâce*. The lights went out. I looked up. The lamp stood there innocent and coy, mocking me.

We finally got rid of the monster. It was the lamp or me. The Salvation Army truck took it away. I watched it go with a feeling of foreboding. I wondered whose life it would blight next.

The two-headed lamp was by no means the only supposedly inanimate object in our household that was invested with a will and a fiendish temperament. We were amused as well as plagued for years by a poltergeist which had the run of the house.

He'd been with us since we first moved in. We knew he was here the first night because he made a spectacular debut. He took my car from the curb in front of the house, drove it crazily down the hill and ran it into a tree. I knew this was the work of the poltergeist because I personally had curbed the car and set the brake.

That was his only really violent and expensive act. He contented himself after that with minor mischief. He liked to get members of the family to blaming each other for things he actually did himself.

In the dark of night he would unscrew the toothpaste cap and squeeze bits of toothpaste on the washbasin. The bathroom was one of his favorite haunts. He took interminable baths, using up all the hot water, leaving rings in the tub and forgetting to draw the shower curtain, letting water flood the floor.

We knew the poltergeist was to blame because we held many family councils, all conducted under Scout's honor, and it was none of us.

Gradually I pieced together his habits and character. I knew he smoked. Once he dropped a lighted cigarette on the carpet and burned a long black trough in it. The boys don't smoke and my wife swore she didn't do it, so that left the poltergeist.

I knew also that he had some sense of charity. He fed ants. He put bits of food on the kitchen sink at night and millions of them came to feast.

He was fascinated by gadgets. He loved to turn things on. He often turned on the radio, the porch light and the water sprinkler while everybody was asleep. We would find them on in the morning.

He ate eggs by the dozen. Many a morning I rose as hungry as an alligator only to find the egg basket empty. My wife always assured me there were at least half a dozen when she last looked.

As I say, most of his pranks were innocent, and we learned to live with him. But he had one habit I couldn't tolerate. He sometimes shaved his legs with my razor.

It was probably the poltergeist who spooked my wife's dressmaking model and caused all *that* trouble.

This thing had large hips and an ample bosom, but no head. I believe my wife inherited it from her mother. It had the figure of a Lillian Russell. It certainly wasn't my wife's size, but it was the only dressmaker's model she had. Perhaps she loved it.

I grew to resent the thing. It is hard enough to live in a house with a *real* woman. An artificial one is impossible.

One night it got in my way once too often. I had got out of bed for a drink of water, or something, and in the dark I ran sharply into this loathsome, headless female thing.

I panicked. I fought her. She fought back. I am sure of that. I managed somehow to manhandle her into the living room and get a door open and throw her out into the night.

In the morning one of the boys crashed into our bedroom and bounced me awake.

"Daddy!" he shouted. "Mama's *lady* is out on the lawn!"

Mama's lady was locked up safely in the garage after that. She never got back in the house, so far as I know. She was even-tempered enough, perhaps, but very stubborn, and not adaptable to my moods.

WE NOW HAVE A NO-CAR GARAGE

We are caught in the impedimenta explosion. It is even more insidious than the population explosion. For one thing, it isn't so easy to detect. The population explosion is everywhere evident. People get out on the streets. They can be counted. They parade, vote, demonstrate, answer polls, write letters to newspapers, go on picnics, get married and divorced.

The impedimenta explosion goes on quietly behind the walls of America's homes, in the garages and closets and drawers. In time it may dispossess us all.

I recognized the danger long ago. But we waited too long to fight back. Now it may be too late.

The mathematics of the impedimenta explosion is simple. More comes into a house than goes out. We can't consume as fast as we produce. But we don't dare stop consuming. It might hurt the economy.

I put the stopwatch on the boys one evening while they emptied the little wastepaper baskets into the big trash barrels for the morning pickup. It took twenty-seven minutes, elapsed time. I say elapsed because on every run they made a stop at the icebox for rations.

This disgorging of our combustible waste occurs once a week. No matter how energetically we address ourselves to the task, it gains on us. Each time the tide goes out it fails to wash away a mass of jetsam that has not yet been appraised or tired of, and so cannot be thrown away.

One by one the drawers of every desk and bureau grow stuffed to the rims with curious trivia that can't be spared at the moment. It collects through the years—lost, yellowed, and forgotten.

When we moved in a decade ago the house was empty and chaste. It was a challenge. The walls were virginal. The drawers were un-defiled and aromatic with the perfume of new wood. The closets gaped.

We not only met the challenge; we overdid it. The first thing to sink forever beyond salvation was the bathroom cabinet. Today it's packed like an immigrant's trunk with an inventory of panaceas, amateur surgical instruments, beauty paraphernalia and, I have no doubt, exotic balms that have long since turned to bane.

The kitchen counter tops, those once lovely yellow plains of glazed tile, have vanished beneath a battery of electronic devices that boil, bake, broil, sharpen, open, toast, time, slice, and give the latest bulletins on the world's descent into paranoia.

The closets bulge with garments too threadbare to wear and too beloved to cast out; with assorted instruments for striking balls of various sizes on various playing fields; with shoes and boots long since gnarled and dried by exposure and torment; with empty boxes from a dozen Yuletides.

There seems no end to this glut.

The overflow goes first to the garage. Every spring, in past years, I've cleaned it out. I knew it was becoming harder every year; but I never foresaw that it would become impossible.

I've finally given up. I've waged my last crusade. Let the garage sink into chaos and decay. I've done my best. Others saw from the first, when we added the garage to the house, that it would turn out this way. I didn't believe them. It was one of my illusions.

I remember, when we were building it, how I discovered one morning to my dismay that the ramp was too steep to run a car up without scraping its bottom.

The contractor showed me how you could easily drive a car in by approaching at an angle. I pointed out, however, that once this car was in, you couldn't get another one in.

"It's supposed to be a two-car garage," I reminded him.

"Look at it this way, Smith," he said. "If you're like most people

I know, you'll have so much junk in there in six months you won't be able to get two cars in anyway. And you'll always have a fine one-car garage."

He was right. Only it was closer to six weeks than six months. We had no trouble getting the old Ford in. But when we bought the little Renault we couldn't squeeze it in beside the Ford. Because the Renault was new, we favored it. The Ford went outside under the alder tree. It was never again to know the warmth and comfort of a garage in its natural life.

Tactically, though, this arrangement was a failure. When we finally retired the old Ford and bought the new Dodge, we found we couldn't get *it* in the garage even when we took the Renault out. We now had a single, small-car garage.

In succeeding months the piles of castoffs grew higher and thicker and more defiant of penetration, like the rain forests of the Congo. One hardly dared venture into the shadowy stand of trunks, dressmaker's models, mattresses, ruptured chairs, broken lamps, end tables, dead toys, model railroads, cobwebbed chemical laboratories, warped carpentry projects and cardboard cartons stuffed with memorabilia for fear of never coming out alive or sane.

Nonetheless, year after year, revitalized by spring's juices, I pitched in like Hercules and cleaned it all out, restoring order and cheerful airiness.

Finally I couldn't face it. I realized the game was up one day when the boys washed the Renault.

"Good work," I told them. "Now why don't you put it in the garage?"

"Well," one of them said, "it won't go in there any more, Pa. There isn't room."

So we now have a no-car garage. We're keeping the Renault under the alder tree, and I have the feeling that it will never know the warmth and comfort of a garage again.

One of the problems is that some things acquired in American family life simply can't be disposed of. They are virtually indestructible, and they can't be given away.

Such an object is an old sofa. At one time we had three old sofas.

One was on the front porch. The dogs wintered on it and sometimes the postman sat on it for a spell.

The other was on the patio. The dogs summered on it. The boys used it for a trampoline. That's what they used it for when it was in the living room, which is why it ended up in the patio. Too much, too soon.

At least these two sofas lived out their threadbare lives in useful work, although offensive to the eye.

But the one we had in the garage was a real albatross. It had us licked. Repair was hopeless. It was mortally wounded in three places and had a spavined hock.

We phoned several friends, casually, and offered to let them have it free. They all hung up as soon as they decently could. They wouldn't even come over for cocktails.

My wife hit on the idea of giving it to somebody worthier than our friends. She phoned the Salvation Army. She didn't come right out and say we had an old sofa. She's too canny for that. She said, "We have a load of clothes and things for you."

We scratched around for some decent things to give them. I don't believe in deceiving sincere people, even to get rid of an old sofa. It's too obvious, anyway.

I surrendered two sturdy pairs of shoes I had never been able to wear. I have a peculiar foot. The boys put in some shirts and socks they said were too small or too itchy. My wife came up with a carton of garments she had been hoarding since adolescence.

"What's that stuff?" I asked. "The wardrobe from *Little Women?*"

"No," she said. *"Rasputin and the Empress."*

It all made a worthy heap. For good measure we threw in a bird cage. For being hard to palm off on somebody, bird cages are second only to sofas. We piled everything on top of the sofa and waited.

The Salvation Army men clucked with pleasure. They picked up the collection with practiced appreciation, piece by piece, right down to the sofa. Then they thanked us and got in their truck.

"Hold on there!" I called. "What about the sofa?"

"Sofa?" said the driver. "Oh, *that* sofa. We can't take *that* sofa. You can't *give* an old sofa away," he said sadly.

They climbed down from their truck, though, and compromised

by taking the cushions. That wasn't much solace. Without cushions it is harder than ever to get rid of a sofa. Then I remembered a murder story where they put the body down the disposer.

I offered the boys a dollar to get the ax and crowbar and dismember the monster. They ripped it apart with demonic glee. We burned it in the barbecue. It saved us on our charcoal bill, too, although some said the hamburgers tasted like a chaise longue.

Anyway, it wasn't a complete loss. We found ninety-three cents inside the sofa, plus four sticks of gum and a Smith Bros. cough drop in medium-good condition. Also, later on the boys made a bird cage out of the springs.

But it was the trash situation that really drove us crackers, as the English say.

"It's driving me *crazy*," my wife said one morning.

"I know," I said. "It's been one of man's problems since primitive times. You know what the shell Indians used to do?"

"They've changed combustible day from Friday to Tuesday," she grumbled. "And now they say bottles are combustible."

"The shell Indians," I went on, "used to throw fish bones and abalone shells out the door in a heap. And when the heap got too big to see over they just moved on."

"They used to pick up bottles and cans every three weeks," she went on. "Now it's only every four weeks. And no bottles. Just cans and metal."

"Do you realize," I pointed out, "that if it wasn't for that untidy habit of the shell Indians we'd hardly know anything about them— who they were, what they ate, how they lived?"

"What are we supposed to do with something like this?" she asked. She held up one of those cardboard cylinders that powdered soap comes in.

"What about it?" I said. "Looks to me like a simple round box."

"It's made out of cardboard," she explained, "but it's got metal ends. They aren't combustible. They have to go in the metal."

"That is a problem," I admitted. "What are we doing about it?"

She explained that whenever she emptied a box of that type she had to take a carving knife and cut off the ends.

"I put the middle in with the bottles and the ends in with the cans," she said. "Do you think I'm being silly? Going to all that trouble?"

"Not at all," I said. "Not at all, if it's the law. One of the main causes of juvenile delinquency, experts agree, is the flouting of minor laws by the parents. No, do it right, by all means."

I got to brooding about the entire complex problem.

"What do we do," I asked, "with the witch hazel bottles, for example, and the hydrogen peroxide?"

"Why, they go with the combustibles, I guess," she said. "Like all the other bottles."

"But don't they have metal caps?"

"I take the caps off and put them with the cans."

"I see," I said. But I sensed that something was amiss here.

"What about," I said, "the little round cushions they put inside the caps, to keep the bottle from leaking? Aren't they cardboard?"

"I guess so," she said. "I never thought about it."

"Well, surely you don't put them in with the metal?"

"Really, don't you think there's such a thing as being too conscientious?"

"Maybe it seems like a little thing," I conceded. "But it's a start. Once you've committed an illegal act, where do you stop? A wrong is a wrong. Next you'd find yourself putting plastic toothpaste caps in with the metal tubes. Sooner or later you'd do something too big to overlook. They'd catch up with you."

"I don't think anybody would ever notice."

"Maybe not. But you'd know, in your own heart. One has to live with oneself. What about salt?"

"Salt?"

"Those round cardboard boxes the salt comes in. Don't they have a little metal spout?"

"Oh, those," she said. "Why don't we just throw them out the door? When the heap gets too big we can move on."

It might be worth trying.

I used to think of the policeman, the fireman, and the postman as the true kingpins of our democratic society. Now I think we must add the trash and can men. If they fail to keep their appointed rounds all would collapse.

It was the firemen, by the way, who gave us our darkest days in this problem of waste. Most men admire firemen. Maybe that's because we went through a fireman phase as boys, before life squeezed us into white collars. Whatever crimes I committed as a child, setting fires was not one of them.

So I was stunned when my wife phoned me at work to say I'd been cited as a fire hazard.

"The Fire Department was by for an inspection," she said, "with their red engines and everything."

"What have we done?" I asked. I thought maybe it was the kerosene torches we burn for barbecues.

"It's our canyon," she explained. "It's a fire hazard. We have to remove all our dry cut flammable vegetation. They gave us two weeks."

"What's dry cut flammable vegetation?"

She said dry cut flammable vegetation was the snippings we had emptied into the canyon from the pruning, mowing, trimming, and unearthing of our flora over the past ten years.

"Why did you throw all that stuff down there anyway?" I asked.

"It was your idea," she said. "I wanted to put it in the trash. You said it was organic matter and in time it would become a part of the earth again from which it sprang. You said it was nature's way."

"Well, it can't amount to much anyway," I said. "What is there—some grass, a dead tree limb or two?"

"You better come home and take a look," she said.

I hurried home. In the summers I had sat on the patio and enjoyed gazing out over the canyon at the shimmering view of our neighbors' houses. I had never suspected the presence of the organic monster that was coming to steamy life just over the edge of the lawn.

I put on tennis shoes and descended into the spongy tundra. It looked like the debris on Guadalcanal when they moved in and cut back the jungle to build the airfield.

I fell through a hole in the morass. Something stabbed through my tennis shoe. It was a rusty nail.

"I've been hurt," I cried. "Help me out of here!"

We discovered an ugly round pink dot on the ball of my right foot.

"I suppose I'll have to stay off this foot as much as possible," I said. "The skin may be punctured."

"In that case," my wife said, "you'll need a tetanus booster."

"No, no," I said. "It's not that serious. I'll baby it a day or two."

Working weekends and after school, my wife and the boys raised the debris to the back yard two days before the deadline. What they brought up created a prehistoric panorama on the lawn. One might have expected to see a pterodactyl flapping overhead.

Scattered among the dry cut flammable vegetation, as if washed up from a swamp, was an odd inventory of weathered, inorganic artifacts—bric-a-brac that had vanished mysteriously from our lives in that decade.

. . . A football, a chair rocker, a tarnished bugle, a tuning fork, a tennis ball, an automobile manifold, a John Philip Sousa record, a pepper grinder, a dead floor lamp . . .

We were delighted at having these things back, as well as to have pleased the Fire Department and restored ourselves to good standing in the community.

But it wasn't cheap. We had to pay twenty-five dollars to get the dry cut flammable vegetation hauled away, and the tetanus booster cost me five.

And the next day we forgot to put the trash out.

THE PARADOX INTENTION METHOD

For years I have had two problems related to the night. One is insomnia and the other is nightmares. Some nights I can't fall asleep because I know that when I do I'm in for a terrifying experience.

Sleeping pills don't help. All they do is intensify my dreams by adding a fourth dimension and Vistavision. And when the alarm rings I can't wake up.

So it was a catastrophe that evil night when I got out of bed and took two sleeping pills by mistake. I thought they were aspirin.

No sooner was I back under the electric blanket than I began to dream. At least I thought I was dreaming. The worst part about my dreams is that I never know whether they're dreams or reality. I can't separate one from the other, even in the morning.

This particular night I dreamed I was being expelled from Harvard for playing basketball without any clothes on in the girls' gymnasium. It's one of my repertory. Then the dogs began to bark. They saw phantoms in the night. They never barked at real evil. While I was packing to leave Harvard the dogs began this tremulous duet. It sounded like the mezzo and the baritone from the *Rigoletto* quartet. I got to humming the tenor role in my sleep and couldn't sleep.

I got up and went outside and smacked the dogs a couple of licks with a rolled-up *Life* magazine. Then I noticed that my old regiment was drilling by ranks and files in the street. I got in my usual place. Only then did I realize I was wearing nothing but my pajama top.

The Commandant of the Marine Corps was standing under the street light playing the lute. Three Harvard girls were turning handsprings with the Chief Justice of the United States.

I went back to bed and turned up the electric blanket. The dogs began barking. This time it was the Rodolfo role from *La Boheme* where Mimi is dying of consumption. I tried humming the Mimi part but it always sets me to coughing.

I got up and went outside and sat in the patio to give the dogs a sense of security. It dawned on me gradually that my wife was entertaining the PTA ladies in the patio. They were barbecuing the principal. I realized I was wearing nothing but house slippers and a Sam Browne belt.

I went back to bed and woke up my wife.

"Can't you sleep?" she yawned.

"I *am* sleeping," I told her. "I took a couple of aspirin."

"You couldn't have," she said. "We're out of aspirin."

"I took something," I said, sitting up in alarm. "What do you suppose it was?"

"It must have been the sleeping pills," she said.

"Sleeping pills!" I cried. "My God! I didn't know we had any!"

"You bought them last summer," she said. "Remember? You were going to put them in the dogs' food so they would sleep through the night and not bark."

Just then the alarm rang. I fell asleep.

Since I'm such a dreamer I've made a study of dreams, not that it's helped me to understand my own. I read once that you can actually tell if anyone is dreaming by looking at his or her eyeballs while they're asleep.

The idea is that whenever a person is dreaming his eyes follow what he is looking at. And as his eyeballs move from side to side or up and down, depending on what he is looking at, his eyelids reflect this movement.

I don't want to knock science. Not in times like these. But I'm always wary of these new discoveries. I notice they are always proved by experiments among so many hundreds of volunteer students of both sexes.

College students, traditionally, are willing to subject themselves to all kinds of weird experiments in order to earn a dollar or two for books, tuition, and corsages. They've been known to steal cadavers, perform marathon dances, squeeze themselves into telephone booths and even allow their wrists and ankles to be hooked up to sensitive blood-pressure machines during the most excrutiatingly intimate moments. For some of these sacrifices to science the students had to be married to each other—afterward, at least, if they weren't already.

I'm no longer a college boy but I have been married for some time. So I decided to test this new theory about being able to see if anybody is dreaming by watching their eyeballs while they're asleep.

After my wife went to sleep one night, I turned on my reading lamp and started watching her eyeballs. She woke up.

"What's the matter?" she said. "Can't you sleep?"

"*I* can sleep all right," I said. "What's the matter with *you?*"

"Nothing's the matter with me," she said, "except why are you shining the light in my eyes?"

"I was going to try to finish *Doctor Zhivago,*" I explained. "If it bothers you I'll turn the light off until you go back to sleep."

She got up on an elbow. "No," she said. "If you want to read I'll go sleep on the couch."

"Forget it," I said. "Go back to sleep. Don't worry about a thing."

I turned out the light. She fell back on her pillow and closed her eyes. I waited for that regular breathing rhythm that would mean she was sound asleep. I waited. Waited. Waited.

"Wake up!" she was shouting. She was shaking my shoulder. "It's time to go to work."

"What happened!" I cried, bolting up. "Did I drop off or something?"

"Were *you* out!" she said. "Your eyes were going back and forth, back and forth. You must have been dreaming."

It was one of my most successful experiments.

A warm summer night can be full of adventure for people who can't sleep.

One wretched night I lay awake until four o'clock, and then

dropped off from the ragged exhaustion that comes of prolonged terror.

I had awakened about midnight with a dry throat. I got up in the dark and groped through the hostile shadows toward the kitchen. I had just tripped over the ottoman when I heard the refrigerator turn off. Then a door slammed.

I froze. My heart thrashed about like a caught fish. I tiptoed back to the bedroom and shook my wife by the shoulder.

"Wake up!" I whispered. "I just scared a burglar!"

She sat straight up. "What what?"

"Somebody was in the kitchen," I said. "They turned off the ice-box and escaped through the service porch. I heard the door slam."

"It was only the wind," she yawned.

"I suppose the wind turned off the icebox," I said.

"It's automatic," she yawned. "You know that. Can't you sleep?"

"Not now. I'm quite alert. I have to keep watch."

I had just tripped over the ottoman again when I thought I heard the soft click of a door bolt sliding back. The icebox turned on. I froze.

I decided to brave it out. I snapped on the lights, burst into the chorus of *Kathleen Mavourneen* and marched into the kitchen. The door to the service porch was open. The icebox was still on. Whoever he was, I had frightened him away before he could turn it off again.

I turned out the lights and went back to bed. I heard a movement in the mock orange tree under the bedroom window, a sound of foliage being pushed aside by some live thing.

Stealthily I went outside. I crept around the house to the tree under the window. Suddenly the tree shook. A wild black form leaped into the moonlight and streaked away. It was the Gribble cat.

I leaned against the house to rest. Suddenly I heard the rasp of heavy breathing and the pounding of feet behind me. I whirled around as two shapeless forms sprang at me, sneezing and slobbering madly. It was my own idiot dogs.

"Quiet, you fools!" I snarled. "Where *were* you? Why didn't you bark at the burglar? Stupid brutes!"

I put them in the house and went back to bed. The phone rang. It was Dalton.

"Jack?" he whispered. "I can't sleep. I've been sitting on the patio looking around with my spyglass. I thought you'd like to know there's some guy creeping around your place in striped pajamas."

"Oh," I said. "That was me. Why don't you come over and have a beer. I can't sleep either."

"I better not," he said. "There's something weird going on around here. I think we've got a burglar."

I found some watermelon in the icebox. I ate a slice and went back to bed. The next thing I knew my wife was shaking me awake. It was daylight.

"You were right," she said. "We did have a burglar. He ate some watermelon and left the rind in the sink. Now we have ants."

One night I had some luck with a method of curing insomnia invented by some Viennese neurologist. Magruder told me about it. He called it the Paradox Intention Method. The idea seemed to be that the human mind is a perverse machine, and if you try to make it do one thing it very likely will do just the opposite, like a woman or a cat.

Magruder said that when I wanted to go to sleep and couldn't, the thing to do was try to stay awake. This seemed a paradox, but that was precisely the idea.

Magruder told me that if I wanted to go to sleep I should try very hard to keep my eyes open. It might even help, he said, to punch a time clock every quarter hour.

I decided to give the method a try.

The trouble is, you have to have some way of knowing when you've been awake long enough to realize you can't go to sleep and are in for a bad night. That's when you have to get up and try to stay awake. I don't know how long I had been awake when I decided I had been awake long enough to start trying to stay awake so I could go to sleep.

I woke my wife up and asked her how long she thought I had been awake. She said "Whmph," and rolled up in the covers like a chrysalis. She could sleep on a bicycle.

I got up and put on my slippers and robe and went into the living room. I was wide awake. Every object leaped out at me, sharp and insistent. Every sound in the house—the kitchen drip, the dog's snore—exploded on my alert eardrums. I stared wide-eyed at the wall and thought of a lively tune, tapping my foot.

One of the boys stumbled out of his bedroom and groped toward the kitchen for a drink of water.

"What'sa matter, Pa?" he mumbled. "Can't sleep?"

"Certainly I can sleep," I told him.

"How come you're up so late, then?"

"I'm trying to stay awake," I explained, "so I can get some sleep."

He went back to bed without any water. My wife got up.

"Is it time to get up already?" she whimpered.

"No," I said, "it's three o'clock in the morning."

"Well, what are you doing up then?"

"Obviously," I said, "I'm trying to stay awake."

"May I ask why?"

"Never mind," I said. I was tiring of stupid questions. "I'm making an experiment. It's the method."

She went to bed. I played a Jelly Roll Morton record and cleaned my toenails.

I got out the *Complete Shakespeare* and read Othello's soliloquy to the tape recorder, the one where he stabs Desdemona. She was absolutely innocent. I played it back. It was a bomb. I should have had my adenoids out as a boy.

The window curtains began to glow with the light of dawn. There was a rattling at the back door. It was the milkman.

"What'sa matter, Mr. Smith?" he bellowed. "Can't sleep?"

"Certainly I can sleep," I said. "I'm trying to stay awake."

In a while the alarm went off. Everybody got up and started maneuvering for the bathroom. I lay down on the couch to wait my turn.

"Wake up!" my wife shouted, shaking my shoulder. "You fell asleep."

"It works!" I cried, leaping up. "The Paradox Intention Method works! God bless Magruder!"

SHE'LL GROW SPOTS LATER ON

The inevitable day came when my family went out of town and left me alone with the Mexican calico cat.

We had been making overtures toward each other, but I doubted that any warm relationship would ever develop. She was the cat we found as a kitten in Ensenada and smuggled across the border.

Since then she had experienced motherhood. But otherwise I saw nothing commendable in her character. She definitely had a paranoid personality. She had shredded the throw rugs, knocked over lamps and vases, shorted the television set, stolen a watch, carried off one of my eyeball cuff links, terrorized the dogs that used to visit us, but were seen no more, and devoured possibly a ton of premium tuna, soybeans, whey, and whatnot.

"Do you think you can remember to feed her while we're gone?" my wife asked. "Or shall I take her to the vet's?"

"I'm sure," I said, "that I'm responsible enough to feed a cat."

"I'll get some groceries for you," she said.

The first night, after they had left, I found the groceries on the sink. There were three cans of cat food and two cans of beef stew. I noticed by reading the labels that the cat food had not less than five international units of vitamin E, but the beef stew had none.

Since they were to be gone three days, it looked to me as if I was expected to survive on two-thirds of a can of stew a day, while the cat was getting a can a day, plus vitamin E. Naturally this situation didn't get our period of togetherness launched on the most amiable terms.

When I came home the first night, the cat circled me as if I was some sort of prey. Nonetheless, I opened a can of cat food and put it in her bowl. She attacked it with silent savagery, catlike, while I heated and ate my can of stew. Meanwhile we regarded each other, at a distance, with wary forbearance.

The next night this primitive drama was repeated. She did make one gesture of friendship. She sneaked up on me and with one swift friendly flash of a paw unraveled the left cuff of my sweater.

That was enough. I locked the creature in the kitchen. I tried to read, but I kept hearing the sound of something crashing. The beast was doubtless up on the drainboard, knocking things to the floor.

That cursed cat had brought nothing but crisis and turmoil into my life.

When they first told me the cat was pregnant I didn't believe it. I didn't believe it the way I don't believe we are going to have an atom war and blow ourselves up. It's too hideous.

"How do you know?" I asked.

"I just know, that's all," said Doug.

"That isn't very scientific evidence," I pointed out. He is a good science student.

"Well, it's true," he said. "I know."

I decided not to press him for details. Perhaps he knew something I'd rather not hear.

"Well, supposing it is true," I said. "How long does it, uh, take? The whole process."

"You mean, what's the gestation period?" he asked. "For cats?"

"Yes," I said. "I guess that's what I do mean."

"I'll look it up," he said. He went to get the encyclopedia. I tried to appraise the full import of this possible catastrophe.

Up to then I had managed to live with the cat under a militant truce. I had allowed the witch her ground; she had allowed me mine. And now, they were trying to tell me, she was going to become a mother. Our relationship would be upset. The cat doubtless would revert to the ferocity associated with motherhood in the primitive state.

And she could also be expected to attack me with impunity. Her felonies would be viewed benignly by the other members of the family, with that maudlin indulgence granted the female of any species both before and after parturition.

"The gestation period for cats," the boy read, "is fifty-five to sixty-three days."

"Days!" I cried. "That's unreasonable. Are you sure it doesn't mean weeks?" I needed time to think.

"It's days," he said. "And listen to this. 'The Siamese cat often has a kinky tail and crossed eyes.'"

"What's a Siamese cat got to do with it?" I asked.

"Why, everything, Pa," he said. "Don't you know the Tannhauser cat?"

That brute! Indeed I did. He was the one, I believe, who had been terrorizing my lizards. And now, they were saying, he had ruined our Nell.

"Good Lord!" I sighed. "A house full of cross-eyed kinky-tailed calico cats."

I tried to remember what people used to do with unwanted kittens. Put them in a gunny sack and drown them in the river? No. If I went down to the Los Angeles River with a sack of cats, they'd slap me in an asylum. Anyway, where do you get a gunny sack today?

"What will we do with the kittens, Pa?" Hope and fear were mixed in his question.

"I don't know," I said honestly.

"Why don't you take them down to the saloon," he said, "and talk people into taking them. The way you did the puppies?"

"No, no," I said wearily. "That's no good any more. They know me there now."

The cat walked in. She padded across the carpet and lay down on a gold pillow with an air of exquisite sloth. She fixed her hateful eyes on mine with withering disdain. Then she smiled. She looked like Mona Lisa.

She had a litter of five. I had hoped to keep the whole sordid affair a secret. But the word of her condition had got around. A number of people had phoned or called in person, wanting to know if the cat really was pregnant, as we had reason to believe, and if anything had ever come of it.

Some of the inquiries were even a bit testy. "What have you done with your kittens?" asked a woman who phoned but wouldn't give her name. I suspect it was the Tannhauser woman.

Others made it plain that they regarded me as an irresponsible man and possibly a degenerate for permitting the cat to get herself into that classic condition.

I have learned that more people have strong feelings about cats, one way or the other, than about any other subject, except possibly fluoridated water.

The kittens turned out an even motleyer lot than I had feared. On the strength of what was obviously a wildly garbled report I had a slight hope that the father in this tragic farce really was the Tannhauser Siamese, who lives down the hill.

At least then, I supposed, the offspring would be cross-eyed and kinky-tailed, or otherwise marked by such a distinguished and exotic fatherhood.

It was all too clear from a casual study of the young, however, that this chicken-livered Siamese was nowhere about when the sordid alliance was sealed.

Instead, I had to infer from the results that our Jezebel's undoing was the work of an ill-favored hooligan who seemed to appear in the neighborhood only when some innocent was abroad.

This low-life bestowed his heritage on the entire litter. One might have expected the mother's genes to make a greater impact on her issue. She was obviously a recessive cat, biologically, as well as a social delinquent.

What maddened me, once the die had been cast, was that the Siamese tomcat hung around the patio with the persistence of an adolescent swain, the very incarnation of mindless prurience.

I cursed the brute. If only he had struck while the iron was hot. He reminded me of Norma Shearer's husband in *Strange Interlude*.

To make matters worse, motherhood, as I predicted, gave the cat an inflated sense of her own worth. Her arrogance was boundless.

I hoped the experience would teach her some humility. On the contrary, she acted as if her shabby liaison and its awkward consequences might warrant her canonization.

Most of the young were spoken for in advance of their appearance. I appreciated these gracious offers, but decency moved me to release all involved from their commitments.

On the other hand, my wife thought the kittens were cute. There is a bond among mothers that crosses the lines between species.

I will admit the orange one was not entirely unattractive. She was the only one who looked like her mother's child. But she had her father's misanthropic eyes. She would come to no good end.

The calico cat's litter was disposed of with what I believe was wisdom, daring, and charity. We put the five ragged beggars in a yellow plastic clothes basket and delivered them to the humanitarians who had offered to take in one or more. It was an emotionally exhausting afternoon.

We stopped first at the house of a little girl named Mimi who had said she would take a kitten if it was a calico. The closest we had to a calico was the solid orange.

"We can tell her she'll grow spots later on," I told my wife.

Mimi liked the orange kitten.

"She'll probably grow spots," I told her.

"We'd better be going along," my wife said. "While you're ahead," she added in an aside to me.

We had two more stops. A Mrs. Wong had promised to take two cats, no matter what they looked like. There are people like that. A Mrs. Franklin had promised to take two if they were both males.

"Everything's working out beautifully," I said on the way to the Wongs. "We've got two males and two females left. All we have to do is slip Mrs. Wong two females and we're home free."

The Wongs were out digging in their yard. Mrs. Wong was ecstatic when we showed up. Wong hung back, leaning on his shovel. He wasn't as sanguine as I would have liked.

The Wongs already had three cats. There were two lean young tigers who plainly regarded our intrusion with malice, and a fat old ogre who raked us with a look of naked hate.

I panicked. There must be some mistake. What would people with three cats want with two more cats? I took Wong aside.

"You must really like cats, hey?" I asked him.

"Well," he said, "I guess I like cats. But not *five* cats."

My heart sank.

"We'll take these two," said Mrs. Wong. She was holding two of our mess aloft.

I looked at Wong. His face was an inscrutable mask.

"We better be going along," I said.

On the way to Mrs. Franklin's I was stabbed by an alarming thought.

"The sexes!" I cried. "What sex are they?"

"What sex are who?" my wife said.

"The two we have left!" I explained. "The cats! Are they males? For Mrs. Franklin?"

She looked in the basket. "Half and half," she said. Women have an earth-mother quality that allows them to remain serene in moments of calamity.

"We're ruined!" I moaned. "I told you to put pink and blue ribbons around their blasted necks!"

"As a matter of fact," she said, "I suggested doing that, and you said, 'No,' and I quote, 'It would look too damn cute.'"

Mrs. Franklin was quite reasonable. She took both of them.

"Later on," I told her, "the female may turn into a male. Fantastic things are happening these days."

It was a close call.

That night after I locked the cat in the kitchen my wife phoned.

"How are you getting along with the cat?" she asked.

"Fine," I said. "I have her locked in the kitchen."

"Isn't that kind of cruel?"

"Not," I pointed out, "when you consider that she has me locked *out* of the kitchen."

"Well how are you feeling?"

"Poorly," I said.

"What's the matter?"

"I think," I said, "I'm coming down with a vitamin E deficiency."

DADDY'S LOCKED HIS FINGER IN THE CAR

A complicated situation arose one morning that resulted in my having to drive the clunker to work. That was the day I finally decided it was time to get rid of the clunker, buy a new car and let our present new car become our clunker.

A clunker is a vehicle that many two-car families in America mean when they speak of their second car. It has little value as a status symbol, but can sometimes be relied on in emergencies.

Our clunker was the yellow Ford convertible with the one white sidewall tire and the broken top that hadn't come up for two winters. It also had a left rear window that wouldn't retract.

Seven years is not necessarily old for a car. But this model was old before its time, having suffered irreversible degeneration of its vital organs as well as a lifelong lack of affection. Half of its trouble, I believe, was psychosomatic.

When we bought the convertible it was already old, but I figured the depreciation had been driven out of it. It had, too, along with everything else.

In the first week the car developed a steady ping. It was a formidable sound, like a baseball bat being swung against an old bamboo stump.

I took it to a garage. The man listened to it carefully, putting his ear up close, as if that sound couldn't have been heard a block away. He said it was the engine. It could be corrected by a rebuilt engine.

The day I drove it out with the rebuilt engine it still had the old ping. I drove it back. The mechanic listened.

"That there," he said, "is your fuel pump."

I told him I had put in a whole new engine to stop that sound.

"Look at it this way," he said. "You would of needed one sooner or later anyway."

He sold me a new fuel pump and tossed the noisy one in a greasy barrel. I drove off. On the freeway the car stopped. I got out and raised the hood and the engine hissed at me.

I had it towed back to the garage. "You got her hot," the man told me. "She's froze up. You shouldn't of let her get that hot."

He sold me a radiator job. She got hot again.

"Probably your thermostats," he told me. Thermostats, I found out, are something like tonsils. Maybe you need 'em, maybe you don't. He took mine out.

She got hot again. I stopped at a gas station. "Probably your thermostats," the man said. I told him I already had 'em out.

"There's your trouble," he said. "You need 'em in." He put 'em in. She wouldn't start.

"Probably your battery," he said. He sold me a battery. Two days later she wouldn't start. A man came to the house.

"Generator's shot," he explained. He sold me a generator. She got hot again. Water hose was shot.

She developed a noise like rolling a ball bearing down an iron stairway. I took her back to the garage.

"Wow!" the man exclaimed. He looked delighted. "Transmission's gone." He sold me a transmission, a gallon of oil, a new top, three tires, and a side-view mirror, plus labor.

She got hot. I coasted into a gas station.

"Take 'em out," I told the man.

Near the end the car began to buck and backfire. This happened once when my wife was out alone in it. She took it into a garage.

"They had to boil out the carburetor," she told me that night. She seemed annoyed. "If I'd known that's all it needed," she said, "I could have boiled it out myself."

Eventually it needed another new engine. The old new engine had got too hot too many times and finally the block cracked. That's the condition she was in when I had to drive her to work.

Lately the car had been left at the curb under the alder tree to gather falling leaves and serve as a landmark to friends trying to find our house.

It was the kind of car that might be seen on most of the mellowed residential streets of America, surrendering itself to rheumatism and rot but waiting faithfully to perform one final service.

That morning its hour came. My wife couldn't drive me to work. She had to drive some ladies to a PTA breakfast.

"You go ahead," I told her. "I'll take the convertible to work."

Her face paled. "Are you sure?" she said. "Downtown?"

"I have no false pride," I said. "The clunker is a great American institution. I have faith in it."

Nonetheless, I approached the thing with anxiety, as you might approach a mean old dog you used to know but haven't seen lately.

The seat, long since covered with green oilcloth, was now covered with a mulch of decaying leaves. Even in health this machine had always started slowly in the morning, like some other members of the family.

It groaned weakly under the prodding of the senile battery. But I had always known how to rouse it. Finally the engine turned over with an obscene burp that was heard round the neighborhood. It purged itself of a black cloud of smoke.

We lurched off down the hill. I had forgotten to notice the windshield. It was encrusted with the summer's leavings. I stopped and wiped a porthole in it with my handkerchief.

The gas gauge showed empty. It had always shown empty. We rumbled into the station at the foot of the hill. I fed the car with my lunch money. Then we ventured onto the freeway.

The car always had good speed. We took our place in the insane rush for town. The airstream poured into the seat and set the leaves astir. As we sped along they soared up and swirled about my ears like wild things. I felt dashing.

We made it to the parking lot in good order.

"Balls afire, Mr. Smith!" cried the parking-lot man. "I thought we got rid of this old blister years ago."

"Not on your life, Harry," I told him. "She's our status symbol now."

She waited all day in the lot for me, with canine patience, probably pining for the shade of the alder tree. But too much had been asked of her.

"I hate to tell you this," said Harry when I came back. "But you've got a flat."

It was the last of the white sidewalls.

I hadn't bought a new car for six years, but a man never loses the knack. Marriage and childbirth are thought to be a woman's deepest emotional experiences. With a man it's buying a new car.

You fight it; you scorn it, you try to escape it. Then it seizes you with seductive perfumes of new tires and fabrics, paints and oils, and you sink into it, drowning.

Finally, after you have paid the price, you learn to live at peace with the thing you have acquired in passion. Like marriage, you even recommend it to your friends.

I had been interested in a certain model for weeks. But I knew the symptoms and was cautious. I admired only from a distance. I grew bolder, sure of my resistance. One day I went into the dealer's showroom, very casually, not looking at the cars, and asked to use the phone. I pretended to make a call. All the time I was studying the car through my sunglasses.

When I hung up I realized the exits were blocked. A big fellow in a Panama hat was leaning against the front right fender of the car with his arms folded. He had a dead cigar in his mouth.

I was trapped. I lit a cigarette. My palms grew moist. I thought of going to the men's room and climbing out the window. No good. The used-car men were waiting for me on the outside.

The man gave the tire a gentle, preliminary kick. He gave me a conspiratorial grin. I tried to sidle by him and make the front door, where there was only one thin sentry. Some inner force took hold of me. I walked up to the car and gave the tire a couple of kicks.

The man let me drive.

"How you like that pickup?" he cried as we lurched into the street.

"Kind of sluggish," I grumbled, hoping to hide the exhilaration that was rising in my breast.

"See how she takes those bumps?" he bellowed.

"Seems pretty rough to me," I said.

"Corners like a pool ball, heh?" he shouted as we careened into a dead end. I hit the brake. He grunted. His cigar flew out.

"I'll have to admit," I said, "the *brakes* aren't bad."

We went back to the agency and sat in an office. He took out a pencil and started doodling on a pad.

"You'll want white sidewalls, of course," he said.

"If I wanted the car at all," I said evenly, "I might want white side-walls."

"Radio and heater," he mumbled, jotting figures down on the pad.

"Look here," I said. "I don't want any radio or heater. I don't even know if I want a car!" They weren't going to sell me anything I didn't want.

I had really wanted a red car, but they didn't have one in stock. "You want the cream," the salesman said. "You want cream for high visibility at night. Can't see red in the dark."

When I drove up in the new cream car my wife was in the yard digging up the bird of paradise again. Wherever she plants it, she decides she doesn't like it there.

I parked in front of the house. In one minute there was a circle of neighbor children and dogs around the car. My wife sat down on the ground and stared dumbly.

"What's *that!*" she cried.

"It's a new car," I said. "How do you like it?"

"You haven't . . ." She couldn't bring herself to finish the thought.

"No, no," I lied. "Nothing final. I'm just trying it out."

"What *is* it?" she asked. "Isn't it kind of little?"

"It's a sports car," I explained. "We aren't getting any younger. It's got terrific suspension. Like a cloud."

"You said you wanted a red car."

"Cream's better," I said. "Higher visibility at night. You can't see red in the dark. Come on. Let's take her around the hill."

"What shall I wear?" she asked.

"*Wear!*" I exclaimed. "What difference does it make?"

She changed into her new green capri suit and put on an orange straw hat with a wide brim and purple fringe. "I don't like to look tacky in a new car," she said. "You think this outfit looks all right? With cream?"

"Lovely," I said. "Let's go. You hold the booklet. In case anything goes wrong you can look it up."

The children and dogs gave way as we went up to the car. I got in behind the wheel and gunned the engine. The dogs retreated to safer positions and set to barking.

"How do you get in?" my wife asked.

"You have to practice it," I said. "I think it says in the booklet."

She looked it up. " 'One must fold and twist a bit to get into it,' " she read. " 'Once in, there's all the room in the world. The seats are contoured to reach around and hold you gently at the hips and shoulders.' "

She folded and twisted a bit, and all of a sudden she was in. The seat reached around and grasped her gently at the hips and shoulders. Her hat, however, had been knocked off. It was on the sidewalk and the dogs were barking at it.

"I'll get it," I said. "I don't want to have to watch that performance again."

We crept down the street. The entire neighborhood had been alerted. They had been expecting me to turn up with a new sports car ever since I got my hair crewcut. I inched along, careful not to run over any loose wild life.

We have a twisting, climbing road on the hill, however, on which there are no houses. It is rarely traveled and is regarded as an excellent course for testing a car's cornering qualities.

I climbed at a quite reasonable speed but gave no quarter on the curves. We hit a beautiful hairpin and turned it like a toy train going around a track.

"How do you like that!" I shouted. "No squeal! No lean!"

There was no answer. I shot a glance at her. Her face was battleship gray.

"It's perfectly safe," I reassured her. "You just *think* you're going too fast because you've never cornered like this before."

Besides, I pointed out, we were going uphill, against gravity, and could stop on a dime if anything happened.

Something happened. A dump truck came rumbling around a blind curve. He was on our side of the road. I hit the brake. We stopped on a dime.

"*Augh!*" my wife said as the seat belt embraced her.

We cornered on up to Ilya Ransome's place on top of the hill.

"I want Ilya to see the car," I said.

I beeped the horn and Ilya came out. She was wearing some kind of Afghan pajamas and smoking a thin cigar. Ilya is the Auntie Mame of our hill.

My wife twisted out of the car. She knocked her hat off.

"How perfectly *enchanting!*" exclaimed Ilya. "Where *ever* did you get it? Tell me at *once!*"

I started to explain that I hadn't really bought the car. I was only trying it out.

"Oh, you really like it?" my wife said, apparently quite recovered from the road test. "I got it on sale. At I. Magnin."

When we got home Dalton phoned. He had been watching us through his spyglass as usual.

"Man," he said, "you're going to kill yourself in that bomb."

Actually, I did hurt myself, but not driving. I was standing outside the car. It bit me when I tried to shut the door. They had to take me to the emergency hospital down near the bottom of the hill. It was my first personal trip to this little haven of mercy, although our boys have been regular customers since we moved on the hill.

They were at an age then when they scorned life's hazards. They regularly suffered minor traumata and had to be sewed up or at least sterilized and bound in gauze. The nurses were motherly and full of maudlin banter.

"Well, well," they used to say, "which one of our little men is it this time?"

If stitches were required, they would summon a grumpy surgeon from his sleep. Otherwise, they repaired the lad by themselves. Then they would tousle his scraggy head with brusque affection and shoo him on home.

In time the lads acquired co-ordination and enough wisdom to quit hitting each other with shovels. Our trips to the hospital became less frequent. The night I got hurt in the car, or perhaps I should say *by* the car, was the first one in years.

What happened was that I shut my right index finger in the car door.

That could happen to anyone. It was dark, for one thing, and my reflexes aren't those of a twelve-year-old boy any more. I shut the door and then I knew instantly and certainly that I had neglected to take my finger out.

I began to dance, I was told later, first on one foot, then the other, in the manner of a trained bear, only faster.

My wife had got out the other door.

"What are you jumping about for?" she asked.

"My finger!" I cried. "It's in the door!"

She began to wail. "Oh oh oh! Can't you get it out?"

"No!" I cried. "It's my finger I type the y's with! Oh oh oh!"

"Can't you get it out?" she wailed again, somewhat repetitiously, it seemed to me.

"Open the Godforsaken door!" I shouted. "I can't find the handle."

She found the handle and tried to open the door. "It won't open," she cried. "It's locked from the inside!"

The porch light blazed on. The boys ran out. Young people love excitement.

"What's going on?" they shouted. "What is it?"

"Daddy's locked his finger in the car," their mother explained.

"The key!" I cried. "Open the door with the key."

"Oh oh oh!" my wife moaned. "The key! Where's the key?"

Gribble's light went on across the street. Gribble ran out.

"What's wrong!" he shouted.

"Pa got his finger locked in the car!" yelled Curt.

"It's the one I type my y's with!" I shouted.

"Open the door!" shouted Gribble.

"Oh oh oh!" my wife whimpered. She began to weep.

Then I realized the keys were clenched in my left hand. I got the door unlocked and withdrew my finger.

"Get me to emergency," I ordered.

In moments we were back in the bright little waiting room, a grim, breathless group. A grizzled nurse padded out.

"Well, well," she cooed, "which little man . . ."

"It's me," I said.

She took me into surgery. The others held back. They preferred not to see.

"Well, well," the nurse said, examining my finger. "We'll have to wash this with soap and water."

"Is that all?" I asked.

"I can put a bandage on it," she said, "if you like."

But she didn't tousle my hair.

It is true, I suppose, that no matter how humble a man's first car, it will always be the most warmly remembered. Certainly I remember my first car with an especial affection, because it was a symbol of a foolish and wonderful romanticism that has long since gone forever.

My first car was a 1922 Model T Ford coupe. It had already had a long and arduous life when I acquired it in the 1930s for twenty-two dollars. It was in this doughty machine that I set out, in 1935, for La Paz, a pearling village at the foot of Baja California.

Wherever men gather these days to talk of great feats of man and machine, my trek to La Paz is never mentioned. Possibly that is because I never made it. But I nearly did, and I think the story should be told. Some of history's most daring undertakings were never undertaken.

Baja California, in 1935, was the only wilderness left within striking distance of Southern California. It was then, as today, barren, hostile, untamed, its lonely stretches freckled with the rusted bones of broken vehicles.

In those days the Automobile Club had a fascinating guidebook to Baja California. It was salted with seductive detail about the trail, such as where one might find water holes, gas pumps, and frijoles.

Poring over that luminous text and its beautiful pullout map, I grew convinced that my Model T and I could conquer this forbidding peninsula, despite the obvious hazards. I realize now, of course, that the book must have been the work of a romantic schoolgirl who had never been south of Seal Beach.

Next I acquired a pith helmet. This superior headpiece was no *papier-mâché* fraud of the type found in drugstores. It was the genuine article, made of the finest duck and lined with real cork from the Malay jungle.

I had now, with my Ford, my guidebook, my cork hat, and the eighty-six dollars remaining of my savings, all a man needed to strike out on a fifteen-hundred mile trek into the early stone age. At this point I was seized by an impulse of good sense. I decided to take a companion along. Two heads might be better than one out there in the bush.

My friend Dalton, whom I had known in school as an adventurer and a scholar, seemed just the chap. Dalton didn't know anything about automobiles, but he knew whole scenes from Shakespeare by heart. He also knew a lot of young women.

Dalton was enchanted by the idea. He not only agreed to put up eighty-six dollars, but also to outfit himself with a cork hat like mine.

My plan was to take the Coast Highway to San Diego and cross the border at Tijuana. Dalton, however, held for going by way of San Bernardino.

"I've got to say goodbye to a chick out there, old sport," he explained. Her name was Margery Bulk, or something close to that.

We set out for San Bernardino. The Model T sang sweetly. Our spirits soared. I had no premonition of the pits that lay ahead. We reached Cucamonga without incident. And there we had an incident. The engine stopped. One moment it was all music, the next—silence. The Model T rolled to a dead stop precisely in front of a roadside structure which turned out to be the laboratory of a lonely wine chemist.

He answered our knock. He was a young man, fresh from Italy, with zealous black eyes and sad mustaches. He had no English. He plainly was astonished at the apparition of two Americans at his door in cork hats.

"*Buon giorno!*" he said at last.

"*Au revoir!*" said Dalton grandly. He was something of a linguist, as well as a Shakespearean scholar.

An hour later I was lying on a pillowed couch, dreamily sipping an undistinguished California Grignolino. Giacomo, for that was our

Neapolitan host's name, was in the center of his laboratory playing *Addio, dolce szegliare* on the violin. Dalton was on the wall telephone, wineglass in hand.

"Have you got it, baby?" he was saying. "Cuca*monga*. Right. Toot suite."

He hung up and danced around the room. He still had his pith helmet on.

"Where the bee sucks, there suck I," sang Dalton. "In a cowslip's bell I lie."

"Hey nonny nonny!" I chanted. It was the only Shakespeare I knew at that time.

When the girls arrived we were singing the quartet from *Rigoletto* —myself in English, Giacomo in Italian, and Dalton in what I took to be a Burmese dialect.

Margery Bulk had brought a friend whose name, as I recall, was Frieda, or maybe Genevieve. Her father had a Chrysler. It was Dalton's idea that we should all go to La Paz in the Chrysler. I was against it.

"Listen," I reasoned. "What are we going to do in Baja California with an Italian violin player who doesn't speak English?"

We went to San Bernardino instead. The next morning I sold the Model T to a junk man for six dollars.

Dalton shrugged off the whole misadventure. *"Wein, weib und gesang,"* he said.

It was too bad, in a way. Dalton's knowledge of foreign tongues would have been invaluable in an alien land.

I still have my cork hat. Maybe we will go yet.

But woman has long since broken the spell of man's mystic relationship with his automobile. The automobile, as much as the ax, the rifle, and the railroad, was the instrument by which men destroyed America's awesome distances and scattered their works and their progeny throughout the land.

In the early days, when the automobile was still noisy, oily, illsmelling, and as hostile as a wounded camel, women were content to consign it to the male province, where it was cared for with a love approaching passion.

Abetted by the designers of Detroit, however, women in time managed to change the character of the American car from a brazen hussy to a fussy matron. It no longer looks like a machine at all, but a powder room on wheels.

This change accomplished, she then took the steering wheel out of her mate's very hands. I realized this one morning when I discovered that my driving license was four months out-of-date. This was more than procrastination or sloth. It was no reflection, either, on my sense of civic responsibility. No man is more law abiding.

The real trouble was, I saw clearly, that I was no longer needed as a driver. Somewhere along the line I had been relieved of this function. Where once the entire family had waited about, as dependent and eager as puppies, for my invitation to hop into the car, it was now I who waited.

I wondered if this had happened to other men as well. The next morning, on the freeway, instead of reading the paper as usual, I kept watch out the window.

One of every three cars, I observed, was being driven, rather daringly, by a woman. Seated next to her was a man—a bit defeated looking, but still a man. He was invariably wearing glasses and had his nose in a folded paper or a book, oblivious to the danger all about him.

A woman who had been overhauling us at an appalling speed passed on the left and cut sharply across our bow. As she executed this lunatic maneuver, she leaned across her husband, toward us, and screamed something unintelligible but plainly scabrous.

"Crazy witch!" my wife said, her face white.

The other lady's husband didn't look up from his book. I opened my paper.

Their mastery is now complete. They have even learned how to curse their fellow drivers.

ONLY ONE FLOWER GROWS

Suburban man's environment is like an evil tropical plant. It grows faster than he can cut it back. It multiplies and prospers. It decays. It has moods. It schemes against him.

But once every year, for a moment, everything seems to stand still. This is usually late on Saturday afternoon. When this moment comes I can look about and see everything suddenly clear.

It is a scene of pestilence, disorder, and decline.

At these moments I know our environment has crept ahead of us on all fronts. I remember such a day.

Even the corners of the new rug appeared corrupted. They had curled up in a sneer, like the toes of a sultan's boots.

The iris in the Chinese bowl drooped like a winded oarsman.

There were five shoes on the floor—an ill-matched lot, abandoned as if their owners had been snatched away by a dragon.

The crack in the plaster had scaled the wall and struck out across the ceiling.

The encyclopedia was out of order. The R book was missing and XYZ was upside down.

The cocktail table was awash with a tide of flotsam like the backwaters of Singapore.

Someone had neglected to turn off the phonograph, now that the song was over. It had the sound of time interrupted. I kept expecting Edward Murrow's tremulous baritone to come on, announcing the disintegration of the planet.

The light had gone out again in the bathroom.

The electric clock in the kitchen was twelve minutes fast. Why? How? Maybe the world had stopped for twelve minutes without our knowing it.

The magazines piled beside the world globe had reached the Northern Tanganyika territory and were destined to cross the equator within the month.

The oranges and pears in the Picasso still life were filmed over with dust. They looked like peaches and quince. It occurred to me that maybe they weren't oranges and pears at all. Maybe they were apples and persimmons. It was not one of Picasso's most explicit periods.

The carpet had spotted fever. It needed a shampoo.

Outside, nature the tireless foe was far in the lead. The grass was brown and scraggy. Bones gnawed clean by dogs floated on its uneven tides.

The barbecue was a black pool.

On the lower terrace the weeds had carried the field. They had sprung up on all quarters in unquenchable multitude, waving their loathsome banners.

In all this valley of blight only one flower grew—a red-orange canna. Its glorious splash only deepened the gloom. It reminded me of a bright life jacket I saw drifting once on a lonely sea.

I phoned Dalton and told him all this. He said it was in my mind. I imagined everything. It was all subjective, he said.

"Look at it this way, Jack," he told me. "If winter comes—can spring be far behind?"

Good God! Spring. I had forgotten that. The weeds would eat us alive.

ARRIVEDERCI, ROMA

Most mornings I have half an hour of fantasy, from seven o'clock to seven-thirty. Then the clock radio alarm goes off. It wakes the household and brings me back to reality.

Sometimes, in this shimmering half hour, I think I will give up everything and go to Rome. I am in love with its ruins and its skies, and the eyes of its women. And in Rome the man drives the car.

Sometimes I wake up my wife and take her into my confidence.

"Wake up!" I told her one of those mornings. "I've got a great idea!"

"Umphf," she said.

"We're all going to Rome. Chuck everything."

"Fine," she said. She went back to sleep.

I shook her. "I mean it! We're all going to Rome. Today. Or maybe tomorrow. I suppose we'll have to pack or something. Get passports."

I outlined my plan.

"We'll sell the house. Give everything to the Salvation Army. I'll quit my job. You'll have to resign from the PTA, of course. Get the boys out of school. Write a note to the principal or something."

Her breathing was deep and regular.

"Wake up!" I said. "This is important. It's a crossroads."

She opened her eyes.

"What will we live on?" she said.

At least I knew she was awake.

"We'll be expatriates," I explained. "You don't need much money. We'll take a little villa on the Appian Way."

"You'd go crazy, without anything to do."

"Do! There's plenty to do. We can climb the Spanish Steps. Stroll up and down the Via Veneto. Throw coins in the fountains. I'll get a vest, of course, and a walking stick, and a Borsalino hat."

"I mean you'd go crazy," she said, "if you didn't have some work to do. Nobody can live with you when you aren't working."

"I'll write a book," I said. "A novel about Americans in Rome. *Three Coins in the Fountain,* something like that. What a title that was! I know I can do it. All I need is the time and the inspiration of Roma—the Eternal City!"

She seemed to be thinking it over.

"What about the boys? What will they do?"

"They can play soccer in the streets. All the kids play soccer in Rome. We'll buy them some short pants and long stockings."

She got up on one elbow.

"I don't have anything to wear."

"You don't have to have any clothes, especially," I said. "You can stay home and wash and sing out the window and make *lasagna.*"

She didn't say anything for a while. I thought she had gone back to sleep. She opened her eyes again. She had only been thinking.

"You have a dental appointment next Wednesday, with Dr. Pragmire. For your molar."

I'd completely forgotten. What a close call! We'd nearly rushed off to Italy and missed my appointment with Dr. Pragmire. Dental appointments aren't terribly easy to get these days.

"I have an idea," she said. "Instead of going to Italy, why don't we just stay home? And you can write a book right here?"

I thought it over. I saw some merit in the idea.

"Yes," I said. "Yes, of course. Why not? I can write a book about Mount Washington. I'll call it *Three Coins in the Birdbath.*"

I was laughing my quiet bitter laugh when the clock radio buzzed. Everybody got up. She started making sandwiches for the boys' lunches.

I put on my robe and went into the living room and looked out the French doors at the birdbath. It's only a homely blob of concrete—a flat bowl on a fluted column—but sometimes, when the light is just so . . .

I dimmed my eyes and looked at the birdbath through the bright morning mist. It seemed, for an instant, as noble a work as the Trevi Fountain itself.

"What're you staring at, Pa?" asked Curt.

"Nothing much, old boy," I said. "I was just looking at the birdbath."